Green Wellies For All

Before the word 'green' had even been invented,
Peter Hamilton was there, getting his boots dirty.

Agricultural college lecturer turned teacher, he
not only welcomed children to the farm, but took the
farm to the school. His boundless energy and
enthusiasm for nature ensured there was never a dull
moment as pigs, turkeys, frogs and all manner of
creatures made their mark on his eager audiences.

This light-hearted account has many hilarious
moments, but also touches on some important
topical issues. Peter Hamilton writes with
characteristic humour (and modesty) about his
passionate commitment to conservation and the
environment. In his part of the world, hedges, ponds
and all kinds of animals have much to be grateful for.

'Peter Hamilton' and 'Andrew Hamilton' are
pseudonyms.

PAULINE
Mc NEILL

Green Wellies
For All

Peter Hamilton
with
Andrew Hamilton

A LION PAPERBACK
Oxford · Batavia · Sydney

Text copyright © 1991 Peter Hamilton and
Andrew Hamilton

Published by
Lion Publishing plc
Sandy Lane West, Oxford, England
ISBN 0 7459 2036 5
Albatross Books Pty Ltd
PO Box 320, Sutherland, NSW 2232, Australia
ISBN 0 7324 0451 7

First edition 1991

British Library Cataloguing in Publication Data
Hamilton, Peter
Green wellies for all.
   1. Environmental education
   I. Title II. Hamilton, Andrew
   333.707
   ISBN 0 7459 2036 5

Author's note
The stories in this book are based upon real life; however, to
preserve the anonymity of those involved, the names of some
people and places have been altered.

Printed and bound in Great Britain
by Cox & Wyman Ltd, Reading

Contents

Foreword

Thankfully the tide of environmental awareness sweeps
onwards; every year more and more members of the
public not only become involved in doing something
practical for the care of the countryside and its wildlife
but by their example and their obvious enthusiasm
become ambassadors for the conservation cause.

None more so than Peter Hamilton, who has written
this book. And his boundless energies for environmental
care, because of the job he carries out, are broadly for the
benefit of young people on whom the future care of the
environment largely depends.

The author has demonstrated that it is not obligatory
to be over-serious to be effective in promoting conservation messages. With particular deftness in this
light-hearted account he spells out so much that is vital
for the future appearance and health of the countryside.

He shows that conservation is there to be enjoyed.

Sir Derek Barber
Chairman: Countryside Commission

Introduction

To encourage you to get your boots on—

Another title for this book could have been *Where there's muck there's magic*.

Peter Hamilton was trained at Harper Adams Agricultural College in poultry technology. During his first lectureship in the subject his interest in children and wildlife, sometimes not easily distinguishable, became known. So he was asked to retrain and start an Outdoor Education Centre dealing with agriculture and environmental studies at 'Clampshire College of Agriculture'. Very speedily he became a realist with muck on his boots rather than a fanatic with his feet on the fender and a bowl of organic spinach on his knee.

From teaching groups of schoolchildren about farming and the care of the countryside on site, he began taking farm animals right into inner-city schools. There, hundreds of children who didn't know that sheep produced wool or cows milk could see and touch the animals for themselves.

Then, from the early seventies onwards, he expanded into sharing wider concepts of environmental care with sixth-formers, teachers, farmers, agriculturalists and students from the Third World. This time he was getting mud on *their* boots, whilst planting hedges and clearing ponds. He developed their understanding of the dangers of over-production, pollution of soil and water and loss of wildlife. But his prime objective has always been to inform the youngest generation. This book is about the humour, the ups and downs, of passing on knowledge and enthusiasm about wildlife and the countryside to many, many people.

If asked for his philosophy, Peter Hamilton would probably reply that his concern was not just with 'all creatures great and small', but with the last line of that well-known children's hymn, 'the Lord God made them all'. Underlying all this work is a strong Christian faith and a desire to share it at 'grass-roots' level. This is a story for everyone and anyone who likes to get mud on their boots—whether out in the countryside, or comfortably seated in an armchair.

1

The Ark Comes to Rest

The Land Rover's engine misfired. I held my breath, but a moment later it resumed its normal guttural rhythm. Then it misfired again. I peered at the petrol gauge through the gloom, for the dashboard light bulb was broken; the needle was at 'E'. Idiot! Why hadn't I made that stop on the way out? I thought we had enough petrol and we were pushed for time, but the snow had meant a lot of bottom gear work. Now what I'd always dreaded was happening—we'd run out of petrol, with a full trailer behind.

I glanced across at Daisy Fairweather. As far as I could see, her face still had its customary calm. She had guessed the trouble, but it took more than a breakdown on a lonely stretch of dual carriageway out in the country in early January to worry someone who'd faced whole classrooms of rebellious kids, single-handed, in the past. She was the former head of a primary school in downtown Manchester. When her flourishing school was amalgamated with a bigger one, she had taken early retirement at fifty rather than go to a junior job elsewhere and she was now my right-hand woman. She didn't seem at all concerned by the thought of what was in the trailer either.

I stopped.

'We're almost out of petrol, Daisy,' I said.

'I guessed as much. What do you think we ought to

do?' As if in answer we saw a lone man, probably a farm worker, approaching us on the footpath beside us. I jumped out.

'Can you tell me where the nearest petrol station is, please?'

'Runnin' low, are yer? Down there, over the bridge, first left. About a mile. Think you can make it?'

'Hope so, thanks.' We started all right and I followed his instructions. To my horror I suddenly found we were on a slip-road leading on to the motorway. I had to go on. Resigned, I drove on down the motorway, but before we could reach an exit the engine stalled. We coasted to the side and stopped on the hard shoulder.

'Lock yourself in,' I said to Daisy, 'and I'll walk down the road a bit and see if there's an emergency phone.' Two hundred metres further on I found one. A friendly policeman answered. I told him our trouble.

'What vehicle have you?'

'A Land Rover with a trailer.'

'What's in the trailer?'

'A calf, a sheep, two pigs, a turkey, a goose, a cockerel, a hen and a snake...' There was a moment's silence, followed by an audible intake of breath and a whistle.

'Blimey! Your middle name ain't Noah, is it? Haw Haw!' He told me to go back to the vehicle and wait for the AA to come and give us some petrol. The passing lorries plastered us with stones and slush so I got out a rug and we sat, out of reach, watching the road. It was snowing again. Half an hour, three-quarters...

'Look, Daisy, there's a house over the field there. I bet it's a farm. D'you mind if I go to see if we can get any petrol there?' After nearly falling into a couple of ditches en route, I got there. The dogs (chained in the stable) set up a furious barking as I banged on the door. The farmer turned out to be a friendly chap who knew all about our Farm School and travelling menagerie. In fact, his youngest kid had seen the show at the local school. He gave me an old can of petrol and wouldn't even let me pay for it. I asked the farmer if he would kindly phone the AA to let their patrol man know that we'd managed to get help. Then I set off back to the Land Rover, only falling into one ditch. The AA man hadn't come so we poured the petrol into the tank. After some nerve-racking moments while the engine refused to fire and I had visions of going through the whole business of calling the AA again after all, the engine grumbled into life at last and we were on our way.

I suppose a reasonable question might be, 'What on earth were Daisy and I doing, charging across the Clampshire countryside in the gloaming of a winter's day, with a trailer full of assorted farm animals—and a snake?' It's quite a story but I will do my best...

13

2
Roots

It all began with my Mum. She taught me about plants and animals, while Dad, though he was keen, had a job distinguishing a female blackbird from a thrush. It was Mum who taught me about God who made the world and everything in it and about Jesus who was my friend. She taught me also those words of Jesus: 'Consider the lilies of the field, how they grow.' That stuck in my mind, partly because Dad said, 'Odd, a cousin of yours being called "Lily", isn't it?' Anyway, I got the message that it was up to us to think about plants and flowers and not just tread on them for fun.

I was born in 1943 in Kenya where Dad was a medical missionary.

Most of my first eight years were spent there and we had a positive surfeit of beautiful wild flowers, including one incredible member of the lily family, a wonderful pink flower which grew straight out of the beaten earth of our only road to the township of Eldoret.

There were also plenty of animals. We had a dog, a Ridgeback (the Rhodesian lion dog)—except this one hadn't got a ridge, so Dad, whose salary was miniscule, got him cheaply. We had a herd of African cows, with humps, a flock of brown sheep with fleeces like well-worn doormats, and a flock of indeterminate hens, whose chicks our resident hawks, whose name I don't know, considered to be specially provided for their nourishment. Someone brought Dad a baby baboon, thinking he might buy it for us as a pet, but he told the man to set it free. We did try, unsuccessfully, to rear a baby duiker, a tiny African antelope with a body no bigger than a rat and little legs like pencils. Poor little chap, I wept tears over him; he simply would not take the bottle and died in the corner of his enclosure one night.

Then there were chameleons with their universal-jointed eyes and long tongues which unrolled to catch unwary houseflies. Weaver birds also lived all round our garden, making nests like loofahs. I remember crying over the body of a beautiful mountain leopard shot with bow and poisoned arrow on a hunt by warriors because he had raided their goathouse in the night. We had rainbow trout in the stream below our house, which Dad caught for food for us using home-made flies. The Africans wouldn't eat them, calling them 'snakes'. This was just as well, for the stream, which was full of them, would soon have emptied.

In the forests around, hornbills swooped, calling, from tree to tree and black-and-white colobus monkeys swung and grumbled to one another. Buffalo, leopard and giant forest hogs, about twice as big as a warthog, protected their territories on the ground beneath. A pair of African wild dogs, black-and-white and round-eared, ran in front of our ramshackle car one day, all along the forest road. There was fear, but fascination too, when a black mamba snake was found among the magazines on the seat of our outdoor loo. A bite in the rear would have been painful—fatal as well.

You can guess that after all this wealth of material on the doorstep, or even the loo-seat, of a budding conservationist, it was a bit of a come-down to have to return to England and live in a flat. Dad joined a practice at Wilverton-on-Sea on the south coast, so that was where we went. But, joy! A year later, we moved to a dishevelled house on the outskirts of the town with an acre of wild garden, and fields and woods beyond.

The garden stayed wonderfully wild, though after a time Dad insisted that he had got it under control. We accumulated a succession of dogs, finally retaining a fascinatingly naughty Norfolk terrier. Two cats from next door adopted us, so the owners washed their hands of them. They were brothers and both distinguished themselves by having six toes on each foot. For some reason they were called Minnie and Tolley, and they were more like dogs than cats, following us on walks up our country road.

But I am wandering from my theme of conservation. In our 'cultivated' garden we had a wealth of wild flowers. We counted seventy-three species of birds there: sea-birds, garden and field birds, migrants and some rare species. Chaffinches fed from our tea-table in the garden; cuckoos came after their migratory flight across the Channel to rest in our oak trees, flights of siskins and long-tailed tits stayed a while; we saw cross-bills, a wryneck, two redstarts, a barn owl and, not in the garden but on the gorse hills near the town, a Dartford warbler—just once.

When I was still a lad, I recorded all the visiting species in the field beyond the house, and later used the material for my 'A' level biology project. We were visited regularly by foxes, for we had chickens and ducks, and one night a badger was spotted. He was on his hind legs eating scraps off a low bird table. On another occasion, I spent the night up a tree on land belonging to a local school (with permission!) and watched a whole family of badgers playing and refilling their sett with fresh grass. The youngsters playfully pulled at the grass and were cuffed round the head by the sow to tell them to behave. They all simply ignored my torch shining on them.

The consensus of opinion was that I hadn't enough

brains to be a doctor. I felt this was hard. After all, Dad had made it and if *he* could, why couldn't I? In the end, having turned down a suggestion by my housemaster that I try for a post as floor manager in a London store, I went to an agricultural college to study poultry. There my rugby career came to an abrupt end when I was concussed badly in front of Dad. He suggested I give up rugger and take up the gentler game of hockey. Little did he know the appalling hazards of agricultural college hockey! Dad's reasoning was that I hadn't enough brains to spare to go damaging the ones I had.

After leaving college, I spent three years as a visiting speaker for the Universities and Colleges Christian Fellowship, a Christian movement amongst students. Afterwards I began looking for an opening as a missionary agriculturalist overseas, but none came along. So, in December 1969, I applied for and obtained a post as assistant poultry lecturer at Clampshire Agricultural College. Soon after I arrived my head of department retired and I took over and ran the whole unit with the aid of one poultryman, who rejoiced in the name of Bill Henman. By this time I had wisely married a pretty schoolteacher whose spelling was good (my own is terrible!) and who shared entirely my Christian convictions. Anyway, my kid sister had already married my best friend—so I married hers.

Soon I became disenchanted with the dull routine of egg production from battery hens and set up a triple unit of battery, barn egg (where the hens are free to wander over wood shavings or chopped straw in a large barn), and free-range hens. Then I proceeded to compare welfare and financial results. These were *very* interesting. Financially all three systems were on a par, aided by the fact that free-range eggs sold at a premium. All the eggs tasted much the same but free-range were bigger and had stronger shells. What concerned me was the welfare of the poultry. It was quite obvious. The hens in the barn

17

egg unit and the free-range hens were healthier and more contented, and I was healthier and more contented in my mind. I hadn't grown up a bird-watcher for nothing!

But I had hardly found my feet when the authorities got hold of the fact that I was mad on ecology and enjoyed being with children, so they offered me a teacher-training course at their expense, provided I started an Outdoor Education Centre. It was decided that I would keep on the poultry work on a smaller scale. At that time the teaching of poultry husbandry in colleges was declining, with the growth of vast poultry enterprises training their own staff.

As I did my course I felt more and more strongly that conservation should be an important part in the curriculum of the Outdoor Education Centre. During that time I did some research on the flora and fauna found on the south and north sides of a hedge running east to west and found some fascinating facts. The variety of plants and insects was clearly greater on the south side and, as a bonus, I discovered in an insect trap on that side a species of *land* caddis fly. I thought this very strange. A caddis fly larva wraps itself up in bits of vegetation and lives in water. When I sent it up to the Natural History Museum for comment there was quite a buzz. It had only been found in Britain once before in entomological history and that had been a fair distance from Clampshire. They wrote back begging me not to catch any more of such a rare insect. Naturally, this fuelled my enthusiasm for ecology and conservation. It also made me realize the value of the hedgerow as a farmland habitat, as this and many other habitats were fast disappearing for the sake of more efficient farming. I felt determined to safeguard these in the future and to work out ways in which they could be of benefit to modern farming.

When I returned to my job in 1971, I was given some unused buildings and four thousand pounds and was told to get on with it. There were other Outdoor Education

Centres in Clampshire but ours was the first in a college of agriculture; in fact I understood it was the first in the country. It just had to be a success.

On the College farm we had dairy, beet and sheep units as well as the resources to study technology, horticulture and engineering. We had 180 hectares of land, some (sadly diminishing) hedgerows, woodland, derelict ponds, and a stream running into a substantial river which flowed along the eastern boundary of the farm. What scope for adding wildlife studies to farming! It was a case of *embarras de richesses*, which Clare assures me means 'almost too much of a good thing'. But I'm a glutton for punishment and I just couldn't wait to get all those city kids to share it with us.

3
'Old MacDonald'

I woke with a start. The nightmare was fading but my
brow was still wet with a sweat of panic. Clare lay beside
me, without stirring. Clare doesn't really go to sleep at
night; she goes into a coma and is resurrected at around
6.30 each morning by a cup of tea. I was glad I hadn't
wakened her. The horror came back to me—hordes of
uncontrollable children of all shapes and sizes, busily
careering round the College farm, climbing into the
animal pens, playing with dangerous implements, falling
down in front of tractors, into slurry tanks. I shook
myself and forced myself to think rationally: the Centre
was going to need very careful planning and preparation.
I reached out for a pen and paper and, by the light of a
torch, wrote down a few ideas:

> The Centre is to be in a farm: not in a zoo with animals
> behind safety barriers, and not in a play-park with
> cuddly trained pets. The Centre is a commercial
> enterprise full of dangers and traps for the uncontrolled
> and the unaware.

> Students, staff and farm workers at the College mustn't
> be hindered by the visitors.

> The children must leave at least as clean as they came.
> So protective clothing and washing facilities are

essential. We have the latter but we must get the clothing—wellies, anoraks, gloves.

We need to train teachers to teach and supervise while I remain the presiding boss. We need duplicated worksheets as well. Though it will be fun, it has to be work too.

Having got my thoughts on paper, I managed to get back to sleep. Before long the time came for us to send notices round the local schools. Would they respond? They did. If not overwhelming, the response was still massive.

At last it was D-Day. A coach pulled into the College car park and a horde of whooping children from a junior school poured out. A posse of teachers followed. I had demanded at least one teacher for every fifteen pupils. They were given duplicated itineraries and heavily underlined *dos* and *don'ts* and I issued stern warnings about entering animal houses or pens unauthorized. Finally, I took a deep breath, and we set off round the farm.

From the start it was a roaring success, but there were one or two terrifying moments. The children were entranced by touching the animals and the animals seemed to love it. They showed hardly any fright. Instead, it was I who got the fright.

We were by the bull pen—and by 'bull' I mean a tonne or so of giant Friesian. I left the group while I went round the side of the shed to gather up stragglers. When I came back, there, despite all my warnings, was a woman teacher inside the pen with half a dozen children with her. They were all stroking and patting the bull while he looked around, his solid metal ring in his nose, breathing out puffs of steam. Whether he puffed from surprise or enjoyment it was difficult to tell, since his face had such a bemused look. We very gently extracted the visitors, and the bull immediately showed his displeasure at being

21

deprived of companionship. He let out a fiercesome bellow and crashed his head against the partition of his pen. I swallowed a few times, took the teacher aside and gave her an almighty rocket, but I calmed down when I realized the bellow had scared the wits out of her already.

We hastened on to the sheep. Fortunately, some had been brought in for lambing and there were several al- most new-born woolly bundles with unsteady legs staggering about, to the ecstatic delight of the children. I carefully extracted one and handed it to a boy of ten.

'Hold it carefully, round the middle,' I said. He held it, as it bleated loudly for its mother, who was pacing up and down behind the hurdle in a state of maternal anxiety.

'Cor!' he said, looking round at his mates, 'Cor, it feels just like wool!'

A farrowing sow with twelve two-day-old piglets elicited squeaks of joy from the children as the piglets nudged and barged their way for positions at the milk- bar. There were squeaks of a different pitch from the piglet I picked up for the children to stroke.

'Cor!' said he who had reckoned the sheep's fleece to be 'like wool', as he stroked the hairs on the piglet's back, 'just like my Dad's chest!' I put the piglet back as he obviously resented this comparison. I wondered what the reaction from the birds would be when we entered the poultry barn egg unit. I needn't have worried. Once the laying hens had settled down, their contented croon- ing made a sound such as you might hear in an organ loft.

Suddenly, to my horror, I heard the only door, which was at the far end, shut and the lock click home. I knew in a flash that I'd forgotten to tell Bill, my poultryman, that we would be coming here last. Pushing past the children, I ran to the door and hammered loudly on it, but he must have been out of earshot. I shouted, but there was no answering call, only a state of agitation created in the shed. The hens were pushing and scrambling around and almost drowning everything with their frantic clucking. It looked as if we were going to be shut in for the night. The door was a stout one and could only be burst open with a battering ram; unfortunately we didn't have one handy. The children twigged the situation at once.

'Are we shut in for the night, sir? My Mum won't 'alf create if I don't get 'ome.' In desperation I surveyed the hen-house and there, three metres up in the roof, was an open air vent. With the aid of some boxes and several willing pairs of hands, I climbed up and, seizing the edge of the opening, managed to pull myself through. Fortunately there was a spare key in my office and we soon had the kids safely out. I got the impression that some were quite disappointed that their thrilling adventure was over so quickly. It would have made quite a story—'Marooned in a lonely hen-house' . . . 'How poultry food saved us from starvation'. This ended our first 'Down on the Farm' for schools. I was elated—and exhausted.

When I got back home that evening I'd just about had it. I fell off my bike in a state of collapse, even though our cottage is only three miles from the College.

'I never knew kids could be so exhausting,' I said, as I drank my second cup of tea, flopped out in an armchair. 'And I thought I was tough.'

'Just try having Jackie all day and every day!' said Clare (referring to our young son), 'that'd sort you out! Anyway, you're pretty exhausting yourself. When we go for walks you stop every other minute to examine some rare weed or bug and you watch every bird that flies over with your binoculars. D'you know, when I turned out your jacket pockets last week, they were full of mosses and leaves? And have you forgotten about that dead hedgehog I found in the fridge? And what about the day I put my hand behind me in the loo for the toilet roll and found I'd got hold of a dead kestrel you were meaning to stuff for your blessed outdoor centre? Really, it's a bit much! And don't imagine just giving me a kiss makes it OK,' she said, turning away her face. 'Anyway, you smell of pigs, though I didn't like to tell you.'

'Sorry, darling, I know I'm a pain in the neck; I'll reform, honestly, I will. But I *am* tired.'

'All right, love. I've got your favourite supper in the oven. Steak and kidney pie and chips, with treacle pudding and custard *and* cream. Help me get the pie out of the oven while I drain the chips.'

That night, replete with pie and chips, bathed and comparatively sweet-smelling again, domestic harmony was restored. As usual at bedtime Clare and I read a short passage from the Bible and prayed together. It was time for an early night. Surprisingly, I didn't drop off at once like Clare but lay awake contemplating the future of our Outdoor Education Centre. I voiced a quiet 'thank-you' to God for getting the children and the teacher out of the bull-pen safely. There was no panic now, only excitement at the thought that we might have started something big and worthwhile up at the Centre. Opening the eyes of the next generation about where their food comes from and helping them to realize that it doesn't just appear in the supermarket, pre-packed, was a start. The understanding that animals are to be respected and cared for, that they are part of God's creation like ourselves and we have the responsibility to care for them was something I longed to get across to the children. And then, it was sobering to remind them that there are crowds of other children round the world who don't have enough to eat. It wasn't all quite as clear as that—just ideas—you get them when you're on the verge of sleep . . .

4

Hockey, Hedges—and Snakes

School visits to the Centre had become very demanding
so I decided that I must have an assistant. The paperwork
was burgeoning and though Bill was fine at doing the
daily chores of the poultry unit—indeed, when I visited
the hen-houses the birds looked round in surprise—we
were now having invasions from schools several times a
week.

The schools' response was coming from all age groups.
The programme varied according to the age of the
visitors: 'touch, smell and see' activities for the youngest; looking at food production and the studying and
protecting of wildlife for the juniors; learning about
geography, biology, environmental science and what you
could sum up as 'Meat and Veg.' and 'Fruit and Flowers'
for secondary-school groups. We were even able to lay
the foundations for 'A' level studies in such exotic things
as applied ecology, genetics and microbiology.

It wasn't long before other colleges were using the
Centre for even more advanced work and I found I was
instructing people studying for qualifications higher, at
that time, than my own! I just had to have an assistant.
The authorities agreed that I had a case and gave me
permission to advertise. One or two retired gentlemen
looking for an easy but interesting job to do in their
declining years were politely but firmly turned down.

Then a Mrs Fairweather applied. Her CV was awe-inspiring! 'Ex-Headmistress of primary school. Main interest: environmental studies. Able to do typing and shorthand. Physically fit, fifty years of age. Made redundant by her school's amalgamation with another.' I wasn't sure about taking on a lady nearly twenty years my senior and a headmistress into the bargain, but everything else was made to measure—typing, worked with kids, keen on natural history.

So it was that Daisy Fairweather came for an interview. She was large and grey-haired but with a kindly face and a shrewd eye and we 'clicked' on the spot. Daisy turned out to be just the job. She was even good at sketching. Soon we had duplicated worksheets, with diagrams of the farm area, safety rules, questionnaires for all ages and guidelines for teachers accompanying the younger children, all prepared.

For any innovation in a community to be achieved without opposition would be little short of miraculous, and miracles are not my strong suit. Many of the Clampshire College students regarded the almost daily invasion of children, small and large, with a kindly tolerance and were ready to show off their interests and skills, but some obviously regarded them as an inferior breed with a pretty high nuisance quotient. This led to a lack of co-operation. Some of the staff too seemed to feel their status threatened by having to answer the naïve questions of little children. Well, you can't win 'em all, but on the whole things weren't too bad. Something that gave our status a boost came in a very unexpected way.

Chris Harris, from the engineering department, came barging into the office one Friday morning while I was dictating a letter to a high-school head. 'You don't wield a hockey stick, do you?' he asked abruptly. 'We're one short for the staff match against the students tomorrow.'

'Well, I have played.'

'Good man, you're on. Where did you play?'

'In the forwards.'

'Even better.' He looked at me with a doubtful glance. 'You look a bit weighty for a forward. Sure you wouldn't be happier as a back?'

'Quite sure.'

'Right then, two o'clock. We'll fix you up with a stick, if you haven't got one.'

'I've got one, thanks.' I didn't mention that I'd been four years in my school's first eleven, captain for two and that the school was acknowledged as one of the best hockey schools in the country. Nor that I had played for three years for Harper Adams and could do the hundred yards in 10.2 seconds. Anyway, I went home and looked out my old and battered hockey stick and had a practice knock about on our bit of grass at home with Clare.

I will draw a humble veil over the match. The staff hadn't beaten the students within living memory but they did this time. Though they could field several players of moderate skill, the rest had let themselves go and were huffing and puffing after twenty minutes. Having a fairly low centre of gravity, I can turn on a sixpence and rob an opponent in a flash just when he thinks he is safely past me. Final score: Students 1, Staff 2 and, I blush to admit, both scored by me. It may have been coincidental, but all I can say is that from there on my schoolchildren got a lot more help and attention from both staff and pupils. Even entry to the intensive units, from which the children had previously been excluded, was now granted.

By the end of that first year, 2,500 schoolchildren had been to the Centre, and my hyperactive brain was now thinking up new schemes. My dad says there is a mental illness where sufferers have a symptom known as flights of ideas. Perhaps I've got a touch of it.

As the numbers of children visiting us grew we knew we had to grow too. We needed to extend the variety of useful things we could offer. You can get tired of just studying the home life of the pig, and fields, ponds and wild flowers begin to pall a bit if you only look at them. Why not stop just looking—and start doing!

I persuaded the College to give me a tiny corner of the estate, about five hundred square metres. We allowed this to go wild, so encouraging the balanced growth of many species of wild plants and providing a habitat for many animals. Nearby we found a secluded pond. Here even the youngest child could catch some pond life in a net, and later look at it with the aid of the microscopes which had been added to our 'lab' equipment from hard-won grants. They saw caddis fly larvae, sticklebacks, newts, minute crustacea and, using the microscope, tiny fresh-water life. We discovered that the area contained rare animals such as water shrews and great crested newts. One of these fine amphibians was hailed with an excited, 'Look sir, bloomin' great yellow-bellied lizard swim-min'!' by the boy who found it.

For older pupils we eventually got permission to start replanting rooted-out hedgerows, after a little incident helped to convince the authorities of their importance. I took the farm manager to see a fine 'A' shaped, two-metres-high, maintained hedge on a farm nearby and showed him a pair of kestrels that had made a pine tree in the hedge their breeding site. He was really overcome to think that the farm development of massive fields meant the end of potential homes for this beautiful bird.

When the children knew and understood the purpose of sticking in those unimportant-looking little transplants of hawthorn, blackthorn, hazel, holly, hornbeam and beech, they were thrilled. Just think, they were helping to re-establish homes for a whole variety of birds— thrushes, blackbirds, chaffinches, bullfinches, tits, robins, tree sparrows, yellowhammers, greenfinches— many of which had been only names to them before. Not only that, but I told them that while they might see cattle standing miserably by a wire fence, their backsides to the wind and driving rain, the cows would be quite happy behind thick hedges. 'If only those cows could say what they think of grubbed-out hedges!' I remarked. The world of the hedgerow was a fascinating topic. One day as I was working with a group of fourteen-year-olds I told them that they might be making history.

'How d'you mean, Mr Hamilton?'

'Let's take a break and I'll show you something.' With great alacrity they downed tools and quickly followed me over a stile into the next field and over to the far hedge.

'Now, walk down this hedge for thirty paces and then another thirty paces and so on, and each time count the types of bushes you can see in the hedge at that point and remember them, OK?' They came back.

'You don't count blackberries, do you?'

'No, only proper bushes.' They had a quick pow-wow and, after a bit of argument, a big boy announced, 'We found seven.'

I began to explain about dating hedgerows. 'Long ago when they planted hedges they would only have planted one kind, probably hawthorn to start with. Then the seeds of another bush came and took root and it would take roughly a hundred years for them to grow right along the hedge. Then another sort would arrive and take another hundred years and so on. You found seven different bushes that kept on showing up every thirty paces, so how old is that hedge?' Silence.

'Seven hundred years! How about that?'

'Cor, Mister!'

'So you've been planting something that may be here several hundred years from now.'

When they went back to the job of planting, I noticed a remarkable increase in effort; they set about it with enthusiasm.

A week or two later we had a different team which was working on replanting trees at intervals along the river bank. It was late in the winter afternoon and I was supervising another group on hedges a field or two away when a boy came panting up to me.

'Sir! Come quick—there's a body floating down the river!'

We raced back and, sure enough, in the gathering dusk I could see, to my horror, a pair of naked legs sticking out of a patch of weeds in the middle of the river.

'Here sir!' One of them handed me a pole he'd picked up. I waded into the river as far as my wellies would let me and feverishly started to drag the legs, tangled in weed, towards the bank. They felt very light. I heard a suppressed snigger behind me as I steered 'the legs' closer and all was revealed! The body was the lower half of a tailor's dummy which, somehow or other, had ended up in the river. The riverside team were splitting their sides. I joined in. It was just the thing I'd love to have done to a teacher at my school.

I told Clare the story when I got home that evening. She smiled brightly but I got the feeling that she wasn't quite taking it in.

'I've got something to tell you too, darling—I'm sure we're expecting number two,' she said quietly.

I stared at her, then I jumped up, swallowed my mouthful of scrambled egg, and gave her a hug and a kiss. 'That's super! Here I was rabbiting away about my perishing schoolkids and here you were with the real news. But are you sure?'

Clare wiped a fragment of my egg from her chin and said, 'Well, I've missed twice and I'm usually as regular as clockwork. Anyway, I'll go to the doctor and make sure, but I'll wait for a week or two, then he should be able to tell properly.'

'I thought you hadn't been taking your grub as you usually do, but it never occurred to me.'

'Well, love, your head's so full of the plants, birdies and beasties, I don't wonder.'

The doctor in Bentwich, the local metropolis, confirmed the good news. Soon after that Clare was back on her grub, though she showed an appetite for the strangest things, such as liquorice comfits! Just then we had a whole garden of football-sized cabbages and even the smell made her sick—she had to go upstairs and shut all the doors while I cooked one.

Not long afterwards, by an oversight, I could have caused my dear wife to have a miscarriage. Because so many children seemed to be afraid of reptiles, I had decided to buy a harmless American garter snake from a pet shop. I hoped that children at the Centre would soon learn to handle it without fear. Off I went to collect it, and brought it home. The first warning I had that the snake had escaped from his box was a piercing scream from Clare in the bedroom. She had had first go in the bathroom before bed and I was now having my turn, luxuriating in the warm water after a tiring day with a visiting school. I leapt out, grabbed a towel en route, and rushed in to her.

'Look!' she shouted. There, comfortably coiled in the upper reaches of our bed, was 'Super Sid', as I had named him.

'He's all right, love—completely harmless,' I said, reassuringly.

'I don't care, take him out and put him somewhere where he can't get out.' I picked him up and he promptly coiled himself lovingly round my wet forearm. I dried myself as best I could with my spare hand, hitched on a dressing-gown and restored Sid to his box in the garage. Fortunately Clare is a good deal tougher than she appears at first sight and at the appointed time, give or take a day or so, our second baby, Jane, arrived without difficulty.

5

It Never Rains but it Pours

Parkinson's Law states: 'Work increases in proportion to the number of people available to do it.' The 'Hamilton' version reads: 'Work increases whether you've got the people or not.' At least this is the conclusion I was rapidly coming to. The number of children coming to the Centre from our Clampshire schools, and now from further afield, was increasing all the time.

We had progressed from those early days of simply bringing classes of children to look round our farm. Slowly and painfully we had written and duplicated a sixty-page manual about the functioning of the College, describing all its activities, with illustrations, question-naires, maps, diagrams, pictures of birds, fish, insects—all the wildlife that could be found (or imagined!). We also introduced the basics of conservation, facts about pollution of water courses—the whole caboodle. This manual now was available to leaders of school groups.

Next we set up training courses several times a year for fifteen or more teachers at a time. These included specialist courses on practical ecology, freshwater studies and the educational value of hatching chicks in school—how new life starts, how quickly animals grow, how much food they need and, above all, how to care for new little living things. We supplied the eggs and loaned the incubators.

By now we were in a position to expand beyond the seven thousand schoolchildren who visited each year. We could provide field studies for college students, talk to groups involved in conservation management and run courses for small-time poultry keepers, as well as the residential sixth-form field courses which we held during college vacation periods. For all this we needed the goodwill and help of College staff. And, of course, there were the local farmers. We gradually got on good terms with progressive local farmers and eventually were able to take groups of visiting farmers and lecturers from other colleges of agriculture to see the wildlife habitats and other conservation measures that had been set up on farms nearby. All this did not happen overnight, of course, it was a gradual expansion, with many hiccups and setbacks.

Even so, while all this was developing another idea was taking shape. I may be a 'bear of very little brain' myself but I seem to have a certain penchant for getting experts to do my work for me. Years of practice brought increasing skill in doing this. Our next project was inspired by an adviser from the Clampshire Education Department. We formed a Steering Committee of experts, including people of great experience in the fields of botany, entomology, ornithology and freshwater biology, to name but a few. With me as dogsbody/ secretary, and with a far more erudite man as editor, we slowly compiled the 'Clampshire College of Agriculture Wildlife and Landscape Management Plan'. This was complete with surveys of our local birds, mammals, fish, reptiles, insects, wild flowers, soil types, local geology, archaeology, meteorology, farming systems, water, woodland, crops, farm animals, and the management thereof. It was a monumental task—but it paid off. Copies were requested from a widespread group of interested parties, including the estates of royalty, and from as far away as Australia and the Far East.

But there was still something missing. We wanted to educate *all* children—but did we meet the needs of them all? As we filled up the calendar with bookings from schools, a new conviction came looming up out of the fog of all our ideas and plans. Where were all the kids from the inner city? The answer was: in the inner cities—not on our campus. Well, if the mountain wouldn't come to Muhammad, Muhammad must go to the mountain. We were not too ambitious at first. We started with a letter to the head of a junior school in the middle of the nearest big town. 'Would you appreciate a visit from the Head of the Outdoor Centre to show the children some live farm animals? He will talk to the children about how animals supply the things we eat and also about how to appreciate wildlife and the countryside. All precautions will be taken over hygiene and the safety of the children.'

To our surprise and pleasure we quickly got an enthusiastic reply, giving us a selection of dates to choose from and ending, 'It will be good for the young-sters to see where their woolly jumpers start from and that their milk doesn't just originate in a factory in bottles.'

So, in a borrowed College Land Rover, with a small farm trailer behind, Mrs Fairweather and I set out. In the trailer we had a half-grown lamb, a calf in a crate, two piglets, and a cock and hen in a box. With us in the Land Rover we had a stuffed fox, a badger skin from a poor old brock run over by a car near the South Coast and, of course, Super Sid, carefully stowed in his box. We got startled looks when we asked directions from an elderly lady in a side street. She suddenly noticed a fox staring out of the rear window and heard a loud bleat from the trailer as we pulled away.

Leaving the Land Rover and trailer in the school car park we walked to the front door. A small boy came out and pointed the way to the Head's office. Mr Grant, the Head, gave us a friendly welcome but asked us a little nervously, 'Now, you will ensure that the children are not frightened, won't you? As I intimated in my letter, the boys and girls have, on the whole, very little knowledge of farm animals.'

'Don't worry,' I assured him. 'We have already had great numbers of children on the farm, even though this is the first time we've brought the farm to the school. We shall be very careful and tell them how to approach the animals so as not to upset them. We've often observed that the animals behave very quietly when children are around them, just as if they understood that they wouldn't hurt them.'

The Head didn't look entirely convinced. However, all he said was, 'We've made the sports hall available for the occasion. First, though, you and your assistant must come and have lunch with us, then the staff and the children will get to know you a bit. I forgot to mention one thing. We have invited some children from nearby primary schools to join in. I expect there will be about three hundred in all.'

This was certainly about seven times as many as we would have on a farm visit, but I hoped for the best. I asked if some of the bigger, more responsible pupils could help me carry the animals into the hall after lunch.

With their help, and lots of giggles and laughter, we got all the animals, in their crates and cages, through the swing doors, along a passage and into the hall, only depositing a large quantity of straw and, I'm afraid, a few pig-droppings en route. We put some black polythene sheeting down on the stage, behind the curtains, which were closed so the animals couldn't be seen. Then we braced ourselves for the onslaught.

In cascaded a mass of children who filled the floor of the hall. I waited for them to settle down and be quiet and then we started, much as we did at the farm, with a short talk and some slides of the farm and the countryside. We showed them the stuffed fox and produced Super Sid to show that not all animals in the wild are fierce. I loved pointing out how wonderful God's creation is. The plan was to produce sheep, piglets, cock and hen in turn from behind the curtain. Then we would let groups of children come up and handle them, but it didn't turn out quite as planned.

As I was concluding the first bit of my talk, the children in the front row started laughing and pointing. I looked round and there, through a gap in the curtain, poked the head of one of our piglets. Somehow he'd got out of his crate. I advanced quietly towards him. My sudden dive and grab failed, he careered back through the curtain and I went after him, yells of encouragement from the audience spurring me on. Both piglets were now out and in seconds the children were watching enthralled as I went tearing after the little beggars as they sprinted round the end of the curtain on to the front of the stage, across the front and round the far end of the curtain with me still in hot pursuit. Eventually Mrs Fairweather and I cornered and restored them, squealing loudly in protest, to their crate.

After this dramatic beginning the show just had to be a success. The children came up in small groups to touch, stroke and handle the animals. The sheep was patted and petted, piglets likewise, and the cock and hen, which had been specially selected for their proven quiet behaviour and pleasure in being handled, sat obediently on children's arms and suffered themselves to be stroked. The hen demonstrated her enjoyment by suddenly laying an egg in mid air which burst spectacularly on the floor, and this was greeted with screams of laughter.

The whole show went on for over two hours and at the end there was prolonged and enthusiastic applause, interspersed with whistles. There was no lack of volunteers to carry the animals back to the trailer. When it was all over the Head congratulated and thanked us and invited us back, all of which I thought was pretty generous considering the pig muck, straw and busted egg which remained behind.

I got home late that evening, completely shattered. But after I'd taken on board a delicious supper of bacon and sausage, baked beans and mashed potato, I'd recovered sufficiently to give Clare an account of our first day's travelling farm circus. She laughed so much I thought she would do herself an injury.

Despite all the mishaps I got the feeling that we were at the start of a whole new phase. It was such a pleasure to open the eyes of the city-dwellers to the meaning of farming and the care of animals. With Mrs Fairweather's help we despatched letters about our travelling 'Farm School' to a host of other inner-city schools and awaited results. In the next four weeks we had a shoal of replies, nearly all requesting visits. News travels fast. Our initial success had been trumpeted abroad.

6

The Silver Lapwing

'FWAG' may sound like a speech impediment but the
initials stand for one of the most active conservation
bodies in the country. The 'Farming And Wildlife
Advisory Group' actually began in Clampshire some
years ago and we formed one of its first County Groups
at the College, following the drawing up of our wildlife
management plan. For a while, that most conservative of
land animals, the Clampshire farmer, viewed us with
suspicion. Were we out to stick our noses into their
farming methods and cramp their style? So I was really
chuffed when the telephone rang one day and a voice said,
'Is that the Head of the Clampshire College of Agriculture's Outdoor Education Centre?' It was the voice of
a real local man and he'd obviously rehearsed the phrase
for it came out in such a laboured way, in a half-Scouse,
half-Welsh accent.

'Yes, Peter Hamilton here. What can I do for you?'

'This is Thomas Raybold yere. I have a farm at
Haggeley Moss, and now, don't you laugh at me, I hear
you're a bit of an expert on plants and the like, and there's
a shrub in one of my hedges that I've never been able to
put the name to, though I've searched in books since I
was a boy. Now do you think you could find the time to
come yere and see if you know what 'tis?'

'Of course, Mr Raybold. I'll come over and have a look

at it as soon as I can. One afternoon this week. OK?'

I'd got a couple of hours free that Wednesday, and, following the directions he'd given me, I easily found the farm and the very hedge he was asking about. Just near an oak tree, which had long since grown out of the hedge to about ten metres in height, was a shrub. It was uncommon, an Alder Buckthorn.

I'd not been able to warn the farmer that I was coming, so I just walked down to the farmhouse and knocked on the front door. It was a nice, well-kept black-and-white timbered building. No sooner had I done it than I realized that this was not the normal thing to do. The doorstep was dusty and a cobweb hung across the lintel to the side of the door frame. I realized too, of course, that visitors would usually go round into the yard at the back where the action was. Still, half a minute later there was the sound of a bolt being pulled, a chain clanked and the door opened about ten centimetres with a creak. A red face looked out.

'Yes, what do you want?'

I swallowed, 'Mr Raybold?'

'Yes.'

'I'm Peter Hamilton. You asked me if I could identify a shrub for you. Well, I have. Sorry, I tried to let you know I was coming, but I couldn't get you on the phone. It's an Alder Buckthorn. I'm not surprised you couldn't find it in the ordinary wild plant books; it's pretty rare.'

'Well now, so that's what 'tis. Missus, she knows more'n I do about them things. She said that's what it might be, but I didn't believe 'er, never 'eard tell of 'n round yere. Thank you, good of you to come.'

The door began to close when a woman's voice said, 'Ask the gentleman in, Tom. Where's your manners?'

The door swung open and there was an apple-cheeked little woman smiling at me. Her husband had retreated and stood shame-faced with an apologetic smile on his rubicund countenance.

'You'll stay for a cup of tea, Mr Hamilton.' It was almost a command.

'That's very kind of you, thank you very much.'

'Show Mr Hamilton where he can wash his hands, Tom. No, not the kitchen sink. Take him to the bathroom,' she said, a note of pride in her voice. Tom obeyed. It seemed he usually did. It was a nice modern bathroom with rose-coloured tiling; the bath, loo and basin were in a darker shade. I descended the old oak stairs, mighty steep and straight, and went through to the kitchen. There was a bright wood fire burning in the grate and through an open space I could see a scullery with an Aga cooker.

'Cup of tea!' There was home-made bread and butter with Cheshire cheese, followed by Mrs Raybold's scones, cream from the farm's own milk and strawberry jam made out of strawberries from her garden. While I was digging into the food, I could see a bird table outside covered with scraps and peanuts. An assembly of blue tits, a greenfinch and a nuthatch were making the most of it.

'I can see you're interested in birds,' I said.

'It's really the Missus. She made me fix that thing up, but I like 'em too. Pretty little things, aren't they? Live and let live, I say,' answered the farmer.

'Look at that nuthatch; I always think it's like a mini-woodpecker.' I pointed out of the window at the short-tailed little chap banging away at the nut-holder with his beak.

'Now, which one's that?' Mr Raybold asked. Keen he might be but he was no ornithologist. As I described the bird, he stared fixedly out and nodded. I was getting vibes that this farmer and his land might be a fruitful field for sowing the seeds of conservation.

'Have you got the time to show me round your farm?' I looked over the table to see his reaction. He pulled out a big pocket watch.

'It's thirty minutes to milking, reckon we could see most of it. Anyway, I've only got eighty acres.' Mrs Raybold came to the door and stood smiling at us as we crossed the yard. He whistled and a Welsh sheep-dog came out of the cowshed.

'You should just see this chap bringing in the cows!' He rumpled the dog's ears, 'Eh, Jasper?' Dogs don't usually smile but this one made a fair attempt.

As we walked round the fields I was saying to myself, 'Little copse here, wild-flower patch in that awkward corner.' He had a very overgrown pond, about half the size of a tennis court, way down in a hollow, where the stock would have watered before the days of laid-on watering troughs. Now, that would be a wonderful place to start.

'Look, I think you've got great possibilities for conservation on this farm. See that pond? If you could spare the time to clear that out and deepen it, plant a few trees at the far end and put up a bit of wire to keep the cows from trampling it, you could have a beautiful feature there. It's a bit too small for a fishing pond, trout and that, but it could become colonized with water plants, insects and frogs, and you might get wild duck coming.'

His eyes gleamed. 'I guess I could do that—even get a contractor to do a bit of excavation.'

We shook hands at the farm gate and as I drove thoughtfully down the lane I could hear him directing the dog with whistles and calls to bring in the cows.

Our friendship deepened over succeeding months and I popped in at odd moments to suggest more and more wildlife features that he might create. He used good soil to fill in a hollow which had been part of a council dump. And, with my help, he planted one hundred trees of various species on it. The Warp river went through one corner of his land and, as he protected its flower-rich banks, they became an absolute picture-postcard scene in the following seasons. I had long since realized that his apparent unfriendliness at the beginning was just a countryman's reserve and we were each as keen as the other to show what could be done—with no financial loss to him, but a lot of hard work. It was amazing what he was willing to do, especially when I realized he was a tenant farmer.

Farmer Raybold agreed that I could bring one of my school groups to his farm to see what had been done and, would you believe it, one keen lad found a reed-bunting nest in one of the hedges where good old Raybold had left a strip of unsprayed, uncultivated field alongside.

The pleasure I got from my visits to Farmer Raybold's was immense. One night I was lying in bed in that pleasant state between waking and sleeping, when I had an idea.

'Clare! D'you think it would be worth entering old Raybold's farm for the "Country Life" National Farming and Wildlife Award? It'll be presented by the Duke of Edinburgh. Raybold really has made a first class mini-conservation area. But I suppose he wouldn't stand a chance against the big boys.'

Clare turned round. I thought she was going to bite my head off for waking her up but all she said was, 'Don't be silly, darling, it's not size that counts. I bet he'd knock Lord Snodgrass and his thousands of acres into a cocked hat! Why don't you have a go?'

'OK, but I won't tell Tom, just in case he gets the brush-off.'

We entered him, the adjudicators came and looked at his little eighty-acre farm and they went away—and we waited, not very hopefully.

One day a few weeks later I was in my office when the phone rang. I answered it. Tom's voice said, excitedly, 'Peter! What do you think? They're going to give me the Country Life Award! I bet this is your doing. Well, if I'm going to have to go to London to get it, you'll have to come too—and Dolly! Goodness, man, you should see her! She's *that* excited and it's all due to you.'

'I'm so glad, Tom, you deserve it,' I said, 'Really you do. All I did was give you a few ideas. Of course, I'd be delighted to come with you, thank you very much.'

We had a great day and saw all the sights, for Tom and Dolly had never been to London before—St Paul's, Madame Tussaud's, Buckingham Palace and the Houses of Parliament. And Tom got his trophy from the Duke himself. Afterwards we had a binge at a Steak House. I was carrying the award in a Harrod's plastic carrier bag, so we stuck it on the table between us. Afterwards I carried it home, up escalators and on the buses, and then on the train.

When we got home at last, Tom proudly put it on top of his drawing room cabinet for all to see. Later a letter came to tell us that the trophy, a silver lapwing, was insured for £2,500. Was I glad that I hadn't left it in the luggage rack!

7
Pike, Ponds and Water-Boatmen

It was one of those glorious summer days, the sort that occur every ten years but may soon be much more frequent if we don't manage to control the greenhouse effect.

To be by the river seemed the best way of keeping my group of sixth-form biology students awake. They were visiting the College for their farm 'teach-in' programme. So there we were, down on the river's edge, all thirty of us lining the bank, with pond nets to collect water-boatmen, caddis larvae, beetles, pond-skaters and freshwater shrimps to take back for study in the converted farm outhouse that was equipped as our 'laboratory'.

To enliven the troops a bit I thought I'd tell one of my dad's well-worn stories. It was one he often told and, as he usually prefaced it by saying, 'This is one of my grandmother's—I fell out of my cradle laughing at it,' I thought it was probably sufficiently venerable for these lads not to have heard it. It's not a particularly good story, but it was the only one I could think of on the spur of the moment.

'There was this smartly-dressed chap sitting peacefully on the river bank with his rod out over the water when the water bailiff hove in sight. He tapped the man on his shoulder and said respectfully, "Can't fish here, sir."

44

'The fisherman didn't even turn his head but just said over his shoulder, "No."

'This annoyed the bailiff somewhat and he tapped the man more firmly on the shoulder and said loudly, "Can't fish here, sir!"

'This time the man turned his head and said irritably, "No!" and went on fishing.

'This really got the bailiff's hackles up and he seized the man by the shoulders, turned him round and shouted, "CAN'T FISH HERE!"

'The fisherman jumped to his feet. He grabbed the bailiff's jacket lapels in turn and shouted back in his face, "ARE *YOU* DEAF? NO THEY *CAN'T HEAR!*"'

The penny dropped and the boys raised quite a gratifying laugh. Then a small voice coming from one of the youngest asked, 'Sir, what was so funny about that?'

I gave up and began showing them how to do the collecting.

I reckoned we'd got about as much as we could cope with in the time allotted and so we collected the plastic buckets. We were just on the point of climbing up the bank when I noticed a green-coloured board floating under a patch of weed in the middle of the stream. The river shelved gradually at that point, being on the inside of the bend, and the stream was slow-flowing. I called to the nearest lad, 'Hold my net for me, would you? I'm going to get that board out before it gets jammed under the bridge,' and I waded out in my long Wellington boots.

The water was lapping the top and a swirl sent a chilly cascade down into my socks before I got near enough to reach out and grab the edge of the board. It was heavy. I'd just got my hands underneath when there was a sudden eddy and a monster pike shot out from under the board. It whipped between my legs downstream into deep water and the safety of a huge weed patch, leaving ripples behind it which rapidly spread from bank to bank.

The boy holding my net yelled out, 'Cor! Did you see that whopping fish, sir?'

I was too busy counting my fingers to answer. Finding I'd still got a full set on both hands, I grabbed the board again, raised it up and turned it over. The underside was painted in large capitals 'NO FISHING'. As I towed the board to the bank, I felt I had acquired a brand new piece of piscine knowledge—pike can read.

After lunch, I wanted to take my students to see another source of aquatic material. There was a pond in one of the least accessible parts of the College estate. As we trooped over to it I began to get the feeling that all was not well: our path was scarred by tracks from the buildings.

We rounded a corner of the wood and I saw an excavator working at the very site to which we were heading. I fairly bounded down the slope and trotted up to the farm manager who was supervising operations.

'What's going on, Mr Carter?' I asked as calmly as I could.

'Just digging a trench for a drainage channel. We've no use for this pond and we can use every bit of land we can get for pasture.'

'B-but Mr Carter, this is a most valuable resource for my biology students; here they come now to investigate the pond life.'

He stuck out his jaw.

I could see that I'd got a fight on my hands if I was going to save this pond from joining the hundreds of others in the county which had disappeared over the last thirty years. In the old days cattle needed ponds to drink from but now tap water could be laid on, ponds were no longer needed. So many ponds had either been filled with rubbish and grassed over or fenced off and overgrown with bushes and trees because the cattle weren't there to keep the vegetation down.

'Well, could you just let these lads have a look at it today?' I asked.

'OK,' he said grudgingly, 'but only half an hour then. We don't pay these men to twiddle their thumbs. I'll give 'em their tea-break.' The boys were standing around now looking curious and their biology teacher, who I knew was a brilliant expert in aquatic life, had turned up and was impatient to get on with the specimen collecting. It gave me a break, too, just to let him take over and tell the boys what to do, probably in a better way than I could.

'Sir, what's this insect?' a boy asked. There was an odd-looking water-boatman flipping about in the debris in the bottom of the net the boy held out for the teacher to inspect.

The teacher's eyes nearly popped out of his head.

'Let me take a closer look at that, Steven.' He fairly grabbed the net, whipped out a pocket lens and stared at the creature.

'I don't believe it!' he said quietly, as if he were talking to himself. He peered more closely, then straightened up.

'Well done, Steven. You've just caught an extremely rare water-boatman, of a species that, to the best of my knowledge, hasn't been seen breeding in this country for the last twenty years! Only one or two have ever been caught. Amazing—we must report this. Meanwhile we'll put it carefully in a container on its own.' Carter had been standing round listening all this time and I could see that, hard-bitten professional farmer though he was, he was deeply impressed.

'Mr Carter,' said the biology teacher, 'I do most earnestly ask you to leave this pond untouched. If this rare insect is to be found here, no doubt this is a particularly fine breeding ground for such creatures and it would be almost a sacrilege to disturb it!' He waxed quite lyrical in his scientific anxiety.

Carter took his cap off and scratched his head. 'Well,' he said, at length, 'I suppose we wouldn't miss this corner too much, but I'll have to square it with the College principal.'

'Thank you very much. I will be getting in touch with the Natural History Museum and I shall certainly mention your co-operation.' I was rather amused at the way Paterson, the biology teacher, had taken over, but the main thing was that, with any luck, the pond was saved—by a water-boatman!

8

Christmas Turkey

When the invitation came to go to a large Roman Catholic high school in the overspill area of one of our biggest cities, I felt quite challenged. Because I am a Christian, I always begin a demonstration by giving a brief talk about the Creator who made this marvellous world and gave us the job of caring for the animals and plants that live in it. I remind the children that we need a proper respect for God's world and also that we should thank him for it. But I had never given a talk in a Roman Catholic school and wasn't entirely sure that my doctrinal knowledge was adequate for this occasion.

The number and variety of creatures we took with us in our farm trailer had now grown. We drove through the wealthy suburbs of the city and then by degrees into the huge estates with their towering, multicoloured concrete blocks rearing up to the sky. At last we reached an equally unattractive conglomeration of school buildings, lumped together in a back street.

'Take a look at those directions, Daisy, and see if you can find out how we get into this place.'

Daisy scanned the sketch map the school secretary had supplied us with. 'Down here,' she said suddenly, as we were cruising slowly in front of what was described on a board as 'St Joseph's High School'. We turned left through a very narrow passage between the buildings and then, watched by hundreds of eyes from the windows above, executed another sharp turn and began hurtling down a very muddy slope into an equally muddy courtyard. We pulled up before a massive sports hall.

A distinguished-looking, well-dressed man appeared through some swing doors at the entrance to greet us.

'Mr Hamilton?'

'That's right, and this is Mrs Fairweather, my assistant. How do you do?'

The tall man bowed but did not mention his name, so I assumed he was the headmaster.

'Would you come with me? Lunch is ready, so I will lead the way.' We followed him round the corner and into another building. As soon as he opened the door we heard the unmistakable sound of a school putting food away with gusto. We were conducted to a table where a small, drab, harassed-looking man was seated.

'Mr Hamilton and Mrs Fairweather, Mr Naseby,' announced the tall man, then bowed and left us.

Mr Naseby had risen and held out a limp hand to Daisy and me. 'I am the Head. It is good of you to come. Please sit down and choose what you would like for lunch.'

He handed us a typewritten menu. Daisy chose a vegetable salad, a hard-boiled egg and grated cheese, and I had a beefburger and chips. I felt I needed a bit of building up to help me recover from the shock of mixing up the headmaster and school caretaker.

Conversation didn't seem to be the Head's strong point, so Daisy and I just concentrated on our food. Christmas was only ten days off and the dining hall was festooned with paper-chains and holly. If the festive spirit hadn't got through to the Head, it certainly had to the school. His table was in a secluded corner of the dining hall, but we could see most of what was going on. Despite the fact that I had heard Roman Catholic schools were renowned for their discipline, and although there was a teacher at the head of every table, I got the feeling that mayhem could break out at any minute.

At length I broke the silence at our table. 'Mr Naseby, I have a good deal of gear and several animals to get into the hall. Please could you let me have some senior boys to help carry it all in?'

'Of course, I will detail some boys to assist, and I'll ask Father O'Leary to superintend them.'

Daisy and I had got most of the crates, cages and bits and pieces on to the drive when a man in a dog collar, with a jolly red face, hove in sight, followed by a troop of hefty lads. They looked capable of not only carrying in our stuff but also Daisy and me into the bargain. Have you noticed the enormous size of some of today's schoolboys? With all the furore about drugs, smoking and contaminated food you'd have expected a generation of miserable-looking midgets. With Daisy leading the way they carted everything in, including a huge sheet of black polythene for purposes of hygiene and a couple of bales of straw for much the same purpose. I brought up the rear, towing, or rather being towed by, Jenny, our Friesian calf. The little priest walked alongside us.

'D'ye know, this takes me straight back to me father's farm in Galway ... That's a moighty foine turkey now, in that crate. Sure an' me Dad had a dozen or more o'dem t'ings, but that fellow in there's better than any.'

'Yes, he is a beauty, and very quiet. He loves to have the children stroke his feathers. That's why I picked him out for this job.'

Up on the stage at last, surrounded by cages and nosed gently in the rear by the calf, I began my talk with my usual words of warning, laying it on thick after the impression I had gained in the dining hall. There must have been five hundred boys and girls there and I noticed, at the back, some adults who looked like parents. I must say they were all remarkably quiet and simply stared, goggle-eyed, at the exhibits. It is an incredible fact that, though they lived in an agricultural county, most of these town kids had never actually seen any farm animals in the flesh.

'Now, these animals are not dangerous, provided you don't rush at them when we let you handle them. But—if you mess around—watch out!'

'Cock-a-doodle-do!' came from the cock, to back me up. In fact he had just got his beady eye on the hen, whose cage we had moved near to his. There was a big laugh from the audience. Daisy and I joined in and I could see the jolly little priest grinning like a Cheshire cat.

'I want you to realize we have brought them here today because they live on a farm, not in a zoo. They aren't just for show; they give us our food. Can someone tell me where they came from in the first place?'

Several boys and girls said in unison, 'By breeding them.'

'That's true enough. But we had to have their ancestors to start with, and right at the beginning we got them from God, who made and designed the world and everything in it. Right at the beginning, too, as you can read in the first book of the Bible, God gave us the job of looking after them—and that's what we've got to do—look after them, both farm animals and wild animals, and not treat them cruelly or hurt them for fun.'

I gave them quite a lot more, introducing our live and harmless garter snake, a slow-worm, a stuffed badger, a stuffed fox and some birds' eggs. They were also shown some animal skulls, demonstrating how their jaw structure matches the way they eat their different foods.

I held up a diagram of a cow's udder. 'What's that?' Silence. Then a boy on the front row, one of the youngest, put up his hand.

'Bagpipes, sir.' There was an outburst of laughter, led by the priest. I felt sorry for the boy, who really wasn't trying to be funny.

'No,' I said, 'it's the milk bag of a cow, where the calf

gets his food from and we get our daily pinta. And this is how it works.' Here I stood up a full-sized model cow with a milking machine, 'And this is how we do it.'

'Now, how many of these do you think an average cow could produce in a day?' I held up a pint bottle of best full-cream milk. A kind of rapid-fire auction took place, with me as auctioneer.

'Two,' 'Four,' 'Six,' 'Twelve.' A lull, then daringly, 'Sixteen.'

'Any advance on sixteen?' Silence.

'Thirty-two pints a day! But, as I say, we don't give it all to a nice little chap like this,' I gently pulled my little friend the calf forward, and she stood looking at the audience with her big eyes. There were lots of 'Oohs' and 'Aahs' from the girls.

'Now you probably have seen a turkey cooking. Perhaps you've seen one hanging in a butcher's shop. Well, this is what it looks like on the farm.' I turned round and opened the crate where we had the full-sized stag turkey ensconced. At this point, I usually lifted the turkey out of the crate and he would sit, quite quietly, allowing children to stroke his feathers. I turned back to face the audience. The turkey felt he had waited long enough and jumped straight out of the crate and took off! He flew just above head height at great speed down the hall and crashed right into a nativity tableau at the far end, up-ending angels, animals, Mary and Joseph and a few shepherds. Only the crib was left unscathed.

Daisy had her hand to her mouth in horror, but the children watched the passage of a forty-pound turkey over their heads with calm interest. I looked anxiously at the little priest. Father O'Leary's face was purple, but not, I realized, with anger at the destruction and sacrilege at the far end. He could barely restrain his mirth. I jumped off the platform and scooted down the middle aisle to recapture the bird, who was sitting quietly among the ruins. The turkey made no protest when I picked him up in my arms and staggered back with him to the front. He gobbled cheerfully all the way to the unbounded delight of the audience.

We now invited the children, row by row, to come and touch the animals and see the various preserved specimens that we had in glass containers. They were astonished to see cattle embryos two to four months old. These embryos had all the appearance of perfect small cows with proper hooves, eyes, ears, teats and tails. One even had clear black-and-white markings and hair on its face at four months. When it came round to the oldest pupils' and the parents' turns I could see more shock than mere interest in their faces. I explained to them that a cow's gestation period is nine months, the same as that of humans. I think it brought the facts of abortion home forcibly to them in an unusual way.

This was the stage of the proceedings when I was really grateful for Daisy's knowledge and experience. She was in her element explaining to the children all about the exciting things they were seeing. But I think even her ease of delivery was a bit strained when we overheard one mother telling a child that the calf was a donkey (she must have come in late!) and a moment later heard another adult asking what the piglets were.

We were winding things up when I saw our new friend Father O'Leary edging his way to the front. He mounted the platform and held up his hand for silence. He addressed the school. 'Now I'm certain that ye're all with me in thanking Mr Hamilton and Mrs Fairweather for givin' us a wonderful afternoon, the loikes of which ye have not had for a long enough toime. And don't ye be forgettin' his words about the loving Creator who made all these things. Now, everyone, be upstandin' and show your appreciation in the proper way. School! Three cheers for our guests: Hip, hip, HOORAY . . . !'

At last we got everything back on board, with the help of the boys and O'Leary. When we had negotiated the exit from the premises and were peacefully on our way home, Daisy and I relaxed in our seats and reviewed the day's happenings.

'If I'd known what I was in for,' said Daisy with a rueful smile, 'I don't think I'd have dared take this job!'

9

The Destroyer

'Peter, I've got summin to tell you.' It was Tom Raybold and he hadn't sounded so excited since the day he had won the Silver Lapwing. 'You've heard of the destroyer?' he asked.

'No, what is it? A horror film?' I said lightheartedly.

'No, no, he's a bloke. Farms about half a mile down the road from yere, name of Easebourne, runs a herd of two hundred Friesians. Always on about how he hasn't enough pasture. Not long since he felled thirty acres of old woodland to get more grazin'. Always cutting down his trees—that's why we call him the destroyer. Well, 'e must have heard 'ow you helped me win that yere Lapwing award an' now, what d'you think, he wants your advice about filling in a pond and draining a bit of wetland. If that don't beat the band comin' to you! I said I thought you would, but I didn't tell him what you'd say. He wants to know what trees he should plant on one side, before he sows the rest for grass. Will you go?'

'Yes, I think I will, but I don't think he'll thank me for my advice. Thanks Tom.' Easebourne sounded a pretty tough character when I spoke to him later on the phone, but we arranged a time and a day.

He was leaning on his gate when I drove up the road— a big fellow, a head taller than me, with a red face and flourishing side whiskers. Easebourne gave me a nod.

We walked across the yard and over a field. Suddenly he shouted, 'Open that gate!' A huge bull was trotting towards us with an evil look in his eye. At the last minute he came straight at me. I side-stepped him and swung the gate open. He thundered through, then crashed over a post and rail fence and began the process of adding to the Easebourne herd with a cow on the other side. Shutting the gate, I turned to the farmer. I suppressed the indignation I felt at the way he had casually put me in a very tricky situation, guessing that he'd been simply testing the mettle of this young know-all before he condescended to ask his advice.

In a voice of studied calm, I said, 'Fine bull you've got there, Mr Easebourne, but he's made a proper mess of your fence. Now, I believe you want my advice about developing a wet area. Suppose we go and have a look.'

He gave a half grin. I could see that I'd gone up one or two points in his estimation.

'This way, Mr Hamilton.' He swung on his heel and led the way across the next field, while I kept a wary eye on the bull. A hundred metres off there was a marked depression in the ground and there I found myself gazing at a most promising area of wetland, a boggy patch full of beautiful water-loving plants and, beyond, a very overgrown and choked up pond, just ripe for clearing out and deepening so it could be re-colonized with animal, bird and plant life. And this vandal was proposing to destroy it, putting it down to boring old grass pasture. Not if I could help it!

'This is the bit I want to drain and fill. I thought you might be good enough to advise what sort of tree planting I could do, y'know, to give it a bit of scenic quality.' I stood looking at it all. It was about half a hectare. I went forward in my Wellingtons across the marshy ground to the edge of the pond; Easebourne came after me. We had reached the only bit of clear bank, when, to my astonishment and delight, I saw a grass snake in the water about three metres off, twisting its way rapidly towards us. Easebourne saw it too and retreated rapidly round to the left. I was standing quite still and the snake must have taken me for a dead tree or something similar. He came straight out of the water by my feet. Quick as a flash, I bent down and took a firm grip of his tail.

The farmer stood at a safe distance watching me, goggle-eyed.

'See this?' I held up the wriggling reptile. 'You're fortunate. There aren't that many grass snakes left in Clampshire. They're quite harmless. This bit is his home and probably the home of other interesting animals, such as frogs and newts. That's what he would be after. All these things are dying out as people drain ponds and damp areas like this.' I put the snake down and in a flash he was gone.

'You wanted my advice, well, it's this: don't drain, get in an excavator, deepen and clear the pond, and leave the rest alone. I'll bet you'll get wildfowl here and you could stock the pond with trout and make a bit of money by letting out the fishing.' (I knew that would appeal to him.)

'Look,' I took a pad from my pocket and sketched the outline of a new pond with irregular banks and a small island in the middle for added interest and maybe as a safe spot for wild duck to nest. 'Here's the sort of thing.' I tore out the page and gave it to him. He glanced at it without marked enthusiasm.

'Uh huh. Well, thanks anyway for comin' out, I'll think about it.'

We shook hands and I walked back alone, leaving him looking at that idyllic scene as if it had been any old bit of scruffy landscape. I felt that it had been a wasted visit. He wasn't going to do anything about it. Oh well, I'd tried.

It was the following spring before I heard from him again. One morning Daisy Fairweather came into the lab where I was examining a section of a rush stem under the microscope. 'That Mr Easebourne you went to see last year wants you on the phone. He sounded urgent.'

I picked up the receiver. 'Hullo, Peter Hamilton here. What can I do for you?' One thing was for sure, I wasn't going out there on another wild-goose chase.

'Mr Hamilton, can you come out as soon as possible, urgent like?' Then he rang off.

I fumed. What did he take me for? Some lackey to come running at his command? Blowed if I'd go! But, out of sheer curiosity, I went that very afternoon. I walked straight down to the wet area to see what sort of mess he'd made of it. There, right on the edge of the pond, a huge drag-line was being operated. For a moment I stood in amazement, then I strode across the marshy bit, ignoring the mud which squelched over my shoes and on to the bottom of my trouser legs, and went up to the cab of the operator. On the steering wheel was the piece of paper from my notebook, with my rough sketch still visible.

The driver, a fat, bearded bloke, sweating from the heat inside, leaned out of the cab and shouted above the noise of the engine, 'Am I doin' this right? You *are* the bloke what drew this plan, ain't you? I'm follerin' it just as you done it, exact. Where you got bends and bumps I make bends and bumps. Bloomin' difficult it is too, never 'ad such a bloomin' caper.'

I was amazed. He'd followed that two-minute sketch as if it had been a surveyor's drawing.

'You've done it just right, fine,' I said. He grinned and set the drag in motion again. I called at the farmhouse, but Mrs Easebourne told me her husband had gone to the nearby market town of Handleford.

'Tell him he's doing a great job down there, but I never intended him to work from that rough sketch I did. I'll give him a ring and arrange to meet him over further details. Thanks.'

The week after that Tom Raybold rang me up again. 'I

don't know what you've done with old Jack Easebourne. All the other farmers round here think he's gone barmy, proper round the bend. He's actually spread all that soil from his excavation over two of his best pastures. Doesn't seem to mind what they say, reckons he'll have the laugh on them before he's finished.'

He was right. Easebourne went the whole hog, planted the trees I advised, stocked the new lake with trout from a local fish farm and paid for the whole job with one year's rental for the fishing.

In the spring, two years after the transformation had begun, I went out again at his invitation, gladly this time. Jack Easebourne proudly took me down to his great creation. The surrounding area had re-grown where the drag-line had damaged the plants, the plantation of trees was already beginning to look like a young woodland and there was a small stand of alder about a metre high growing on the island.

'Look at that then,' said Easebourne. There, on the edge of the island, a moorhen had made a nest and there were four little chicks sculling around the water after their mum. But his moment of triumph was short-lived. Easebourne's Jack Russell had accompanied us most of the way on our expedition. Before we could stop him, he had plunged in from the other side of the lake and was now paddling steadily across towards the little family of water birds.

Jack stared at him in horror, then he let out a stentorian bellow, 'Scrimper! SCRIMPER! Come back 'ere, ye varmint! Come back I say!' The little dog took not the slightest bit of notice but continued his paddling more furiously.

'Ah yuh . . . stop it!' The air was rapidly turning blue with Jack's expletives.

He rushed round the edge, stopped and picked up some great lumps of clay left from the digging two years before. He hurled them furiously at his errant terrier with pretty fair accuracy. But, undeterred, the dog reached the island where the moorhen and chicks had retreated. Right before our eyes, he seized first the adult moorhen and tore it to pieces and then the chicks and ate them one by one. Having completed his evil work, he stood obstinately on the island and refused all commands and blandishments to get him to return. I've no doubt he knew he'd got it coming to him.

Jack Easebourne was beside himself with fury and shouted himself hoarse before giving up and walking back to the house with me, muttering horrible imprecations under his breath. In the increasing distance we could still faintly hear that rotten little dog, yelping with renewed excitement as he chased the other moorhen, which was letting out terrified cries. I pictured it darting through the alders and taking off to safety on the mainland, as far away as it could get from the evil Scrimper.

Despite this sad setback, Farmer Easebourne *had* carried out a real piece of conservation work and shown that the results could be both beautiful and profitable. I gave him a few weeks to get over his frustration and disappointment right in his moment of triumph, before asking him if I could bring out a group of farmers and landowners on a visit. They were taking part in a course I was running at the Centre on the subject of 'Creating Wildlife Habitats'.

Easebourne was enthusiastic. On the afternoon we had arranged, a party of about thirty arrived at the farm in their cars and Land Rovers. I gave them my usual talk about walking quietly and only talking in whispers and off we went with Jack across the meadows. As we came round the last hedge I spotted a magnificent heron standing by the side of the lake in a few centimetres of water. Instantly, I held up my hand and the party stopped in perfect silence. I explained that it was a real achievement to have attracted a heron to a new stretch of water so soon and told them to take a good look at it through their binoculars. Jack sidled over and nudged me in the ribs.

'Mr Hamilton, yon's only a plastic heron. I put it there to keep the fish away from the edge so's a real heron don't spear 'em.'

It was strange, I felt the day had suddenly become excruciatingly warm.

10
Water Courses

'Boss, reckon you'd better go and take a look at what I've just seen.' I couldn't get Bill Henman to stop calling me 'Boss'. I much preferred to be simply 'Peter' or even 'Pete'.

'What's up, Bill?' I enquired.

'It was as I come over the bridge on me bike, I spotted it. Bloomin' mess the River Warp looks.'

'OK, give me time to finish this letter.' I finished dictating an enquiry to the poultry-food manufacturers for Mrs Fairweather to type and put the dictaphone down. Then I picked up my wellies from the corner and went outside where Bill was standing. Although his job was almost entirely in the poultry unit he took an interest in all the other activities of the Outdoor Centre. I wondered what he was on about.

'As I said, it was as I come over the bridge an' 'ad a check at the water. It was looking real nasty, dirty brown discoloration and I spotted two dead fish—brown trout— washed up on to the side. Nasty smell comin' off the water too. 'Adn't bothered to look for a week or two.'

'Thanks, Bill. I'll go over there straightaway and take a look.'

He nodded, put a finger to his cap in salute and went off in the direction of the poultry sheds. That was another thing—I couldn't break him of this habit, which suggested a servility which he didn't feel and I hated.

I walked down to the river. There was a most peculiar discoloration of the water, a sort of greyish-brown cloudiness, and a nasty sewagey smell. There were no dead fish now. Probably some predator, perhaps a fox who liked his grub nice and high, had removed them.

I walked up the bank and twenty-five paces on I found the source. A filthy stream of water was pouring out of one of the College drainage ditches into the main stream. Upstream of the ditch the water was clear. There had been a row between the College and the Clampshire Water Authority a while back when slurry from the milking sheds had leaked into the ditch. However, since then the farm manager had enlarged the slurry lagoon and the trouble had stopped; not completely perhaps, but the pollution had been reduced to reasonable levels. Now here we were, back at square one.

As luck would have it, we had a fifth-form group from Bentwich Comprehensive coming on a farm trip that afternoon. This would be a great opportunity to make the best of a bad job and get them to help monitor the water for the effects of the spillage. When fifteen keen students arrived at two o'clock I got them kitted out in wellies and down we went to the river with hand nets.

'Notice anything about the water, lads?' I looked expectantly at the group lining the bank.

'Bloomin' pong!' said one ginger-haired boy. There was a burst of laughter.

I joined in. 'Good lad, hole in one. Now, anything else?'

There was a moment's silence, then Ginger piped up again, 'Water looks real mucky.'

'Right. Now, does anybody know what's causing the smell and the cloudiness of the water?' I could see Ginger opening his mouth.

'Someone else; any ideas?' A bright-faced boy, the smallest of the group, put up his hand. I nodded to him.

'Some pollution's coming into the river from some-where, sir.'

'You're dead right. Now let's see if we can find it. It's got to be upstream, so get going.'

With a bit of larking about they moved off upstream, studying the banks and the water like a pack of hounds looking for an otter's holt. (Sadly we have no otters. The last one to be spotted was seen, I have been told, some twenty years previously.)

In less than a minute there was a yell. 'Here, sir!'

I joined them at the opening of the College drainage ditch. 'Right, now we've got the point of entry. Let's try to track down where the muck's getting into the ditch.'

I myself didn't yet know the source, as I hadn't had time to search that morning. Anyway, it wasn't all that easy in such an overgrown waterway. If we did find the entry I wasn't going to tell them where it was coming from. I wanted a quiet talk with the manager first. The lads had got long twigs from scrubby bushes along the bank and were busily poking and prodding along the edge.

'Got it!' There was a shout and we all congregated where one of the boys was standing. He had industri-ously hooked out the water weeds and established that the stream was clear above where he stood. A pipe exuding filthy, evil-smelling sludge entered the stream there—on the opposite bank. It wasn't coming from the College slurry tanks at all. I gave a quiet whistle of relief. I hadn't been looking forward to telling the manager that he was ruining the river water all over again. No, this pipe ran under one of our fields and on to the land and buildings of our next-door neighbour, Joe Wellstanding. He was notorious as one of the dirtiest farmers around. He certainly didn't deserve his name. His local one was unrepeatable.

I congratulated the boy, who blushed with pride. I guessed that perhaps he wasn't particularly prominent in his class and this could be an unexpected boost to his standing among his mates.

'Now, the next thing is to analyze how much damage has been done to the river. You see, when sewage, whether it's from cattle or humans, gets into clean river water, apart from directly poisoning water life, it eventually de-oxygenates the water. Water animals can't live without oxygen and so they die out.

'I remember a pond at the back of our house where cattle muck got in during a drought. The fish began swimming around on the surface literally gulping for air. D'you know, we waded in with landing nets and literally lifted out about eight big fish—bream and perch. We popped 'em into our garden pond, which had lots of oxygenating plants in it. They all revived and, when the rain came and the other pond got healthy again, we put 'em back.

'Now we've already found two dead trout in the river here, so we're going to see how the other small water animals are getting on. We'll think about how to solve the problem when you come again next week. I'm afraid only one or two of you can collect the specimens, so let's go back to the river and I'll show you how we do it.'

I got them 'kick sampling' above and below the entry of the pollution into the river. This meant standing in the water, doing a quick shuffle with both feet in the mud on the bottom, and collecting any disturbed material and water life just below the disturbance. Each catch from the fine collecting nets was them emptied into a different small tray of clear water. We took equally-sized samples from above and below the pollution source, examined them and did a species count. The sample from *above* the drainage ditch had three hundred animals and eight different species, whereas the sample from *below* had only ten animals and two species. This gave us what's called a 'Biotic Index'.

When the boys had written up their afternoon's work,

had some tea in the College cafeteria and departed, I sat in the office debating my best course of action. I knew that some keen-sighted anglers would be around at the weekend and a complaint would be made to the Water Authority by the club secretary. It wouldn't be long before Joe Wellstanding wouldn't be standing so well. Mrs Fairweather eventually managed to get through to his wife on the phone. Although Mrs Wellstanding wasn't very enthusiastic about my coming, it was arranged that Joe Wellstanding would be on the farm for a chat next morning.

Joe was waiting for me in the yard when I walked in on the dot of nine-thirty. I was wondering what sort of reception I'd get, but to my surprise and relief he was quite cordial.

'Ah think ah can guess what ye've coom about,' he greeted me. He wasn't a Clampshire man. He came, I think, from Yorkshire.

'It'll be about cow muck from my byre messin' oop the Warp, an't it? Well ah know'd it. There's a crack in t' sloory tank an' it's lakin' into t' drains. Ah'll stop't oop quick's ah can, yon's best ah can do.'

'Well, I was coming to let you know, Mr Wellstanding. I'm sure you'll do your best. It is affecting the Warp rather badly already, one or two dead trout around. Meantime I'll get some boys who're doing a course with me to help with a rescue job on the ditch.'

He stuck out his jaw and nodded agreement. Not a loquacious man, Joe Wellstanding. I'd got a scheme in mind; just the job for the boys from Bentwich Comprehensive. All boys like mucking about in water, even fifth-years.

A week later I was back on the bank of our drainage ditch with my team of fifth-year boys. With Bill's help we'd lugged half a dozen old railway sleepers over in the College Land Rover. Now they lay in a pile.

'Now everybody, keep quiet a minute. Here's the plan.

If we can get water tumbling down even small waterfalls, it'll help to re-oxygenate it. So we're going to build three waterfalls.'

'Yippee!' A not quite *sotto voce* comment from Ginger. With spades we dug out three nice little beds in the banks on both sides of the ditch, at intervals of thirty metres. Fortunately there was quite a good fall—at least a metre—in level between the point where Wellstanding's pipe emptied into the stream bed and the exit into the Warp. Half a dozen boys and I manhandled the sleepers to lay them on the stream bed and then dragged other sleepers and placed them on top. By the time we had finished, we had three little dams built up one after another with settling pools between them, overflowing in satisfactory waterfalls.

Twelve weeks later we did further estimations by kick-sampling of the river invertebrates below the drainage ditch and the numbers were appreciably higher than before. The re-oxygenation was beginning to work, even though Wellstanding's slurry tank repair hadn't yet been effected . . .

11
Awards and Alarms

One day in the office Daisy came to me with the local paper. She showed me a small paragraph about something called the 'Mersey Basin Campaign Award', a prize offered for the best bit of conservation work done by young people and schools in the area. I went home and talked it over with Clare that night. Her advice is nearly always sound and so I decided to enter the Bentwich Comprehensive for it.

Over the years they had worked under my direction and replanted literally miles of ploughed-up hedgerows on the College farm. This had not only changed the look of the place for the better but had also resulted in an increase in bird life.

I even carried out a prolonged controlled experiment to show that the shelter the hedges gave had actually brought about an increase in milk-yield from the cows pastured in the fields. Those cows in hedged fields spent less time just standing, cold and wet, with their backs to the wind than those in fields divided only by wire fencing. The cows in the hedged fields therefore grazed more efficiently and produced more milk.

The initial cost of planting and maintaining hedges was greater than that of providing wire. However, in the long run the value of the milk-yield, I calculated, would more than offset this.

The boys had also helped me dig out several overgrown, silted-up ponds on the estate which were now flourishing wildlife habitats. So Bentwich Comprehensive had three strings to their bow: they had carried out hedge restoration; reclaimed ponds and now they had improved the health of a river. We began to be even more hopeful when a photographer came out to take pictures of their work. Several weeks later the results of the competition were announced, and—Bentwich Comprehensive Fifth Form had won!

Daisy Fairweather and I were toasting their success with our morning cups of coffee when there was a knock on the door and in came Bill Henman. One look at his face was enough; he was the harbinger of further disaster.

'Mr Hamilton,' he said in sepulchral tones, 'Mr Hamilton, will you come down to the barn egg shed, please?' I knew then that something must be really wrong for Bill to have dropped his customary 'Boss'.

'What's the trouble, Bill?' We were out of the building and standing on the doorstep. I saw Bill had dropped the body of a hen there. He pointed to it. If that was what he was looking so grim about I was still a bit mystified. We had occasional casualties; it was par for the course. Egg prolapse was common cause of sudden death in a previously healthy bird. Then I had a nasty thought. Bill had asked me to come to the poultry house. What was going on? It *must* be bad. Bill found his voice.

'Fifteen dead, and several others looking pretty sick, staggerin' about, tails all down.'

I took a deep breath. We'd been continuing our controlled experiment, measuring egg production, food consumption, general health and financial returns with laying birds in different conditions—battery, barn egg and free range. Things were changing, but with a premium still on the sale of free-range eggs, we were just about breaking even. This was going to throw our results out. We'd got to discover the cause, before the whole flock was decimated. Bill was right, about another dozen hens were obviously groggy.

'Have the barn egg birds had any different feedstuffs from the others?'

'No, Boss, only we started a new batch of meal, same make as the others are 'avin, this mornin'.'

'Don't give them of any more of that batch, and we'll have it analyzed.'

The odd thing was that the cage birds and the free-range were as right as rain and they'd all had the same make of meal. I rang the firm producing the poultry meal straight away. No, they'd had no other complaints, in fact they'd never had any query about any of their poultry food before. They sounded pretty belligerent, implying that if there was anything wrong it certainly wasn't down to them, but probably to our mismanagement. I got annoyed and told them I was getting the food examined by experts and if there was anything wrong they would be hearing from me. I rang off. It took ten days for the lab to come up with a report on the sample I sent. Result: absolutely no contaminants whatsoever.

Then some of our main customers started complaining about the peculiar taste of the eggs and stopped their orders.

I was getting pretty desperate. We moved the birds to a different shed and cleaned out all the old shavings in case there was some infection harboured in them. The veterinary report on the dead birds was simply, 'signs of toxicity in the liver, crops show presence of a chemical insecticide'. Wait a minute, wasn't that particular chemical the stuff used to treat tree trunks to prevent wood-borers? And the birds were on a litter of woodshavings from a big timber yard. A lab report on the shavings showed insecticide residues. We'd got it. Stone-cold proof!

I phoned the timber company. They were cagey but, in the end, they admitted that they had been treating their standing timber with that particular insecticide.

I told them I would be making a formal claim for compensation and that they must inform all their egg-producing customers with hens on deep litter. In any case, I would have to inform the Ministry of Agriculture. They didn't like that one little bit and cut the conversation.

The Ministry was extremely grateful for the information and said they would issue an immediate warning in their publications, but they were rather doubtful about my getting compensation.

We didn't. Sometimes you just have to carry your loss. As Bill said, with simple sagacity, 'Boss, you win some and you lose some. After all, we did get the Award, didn't we?'

I liked that 'we'.

12
Special Delivery

After that minor disaster with the poultry unit, I needed a bit of a pick-me-up and I hadn't long to wait.

'I think you will be pleased with this,' said Daisy Fairweather, handing me a letter in the morning's post. It was from the National Adviser of the Farming and Wildlife Advisory Group, and read, 'You will be glad to know that we have finally selected the Clampshire Agricultural College as our venue for this year's National Wildlife Conference.'

The theme was to be 'Wetlands': the delegates would be looking at marsh and freshwater habitats for birds, plants and fish. The wetlands question was one I was delighted to tackle. As more and more wetlands were being drained, polluted by fertilizers and weed killers, many rare and interesting wetland species were dying out.

I waved the letter triumphantly across the table at Daisy. As secretary of the steering committee of Clampshire FWAG I felt honoured. All sorts of public bodies supported the group. The Ministry of Agriculture, Fisheries and Food, the Royal Society for the Protection of Birds and the Royal Society of Nature Conservation were numbered among its supporters. However, to pay me back for landing such a prestigious catch, I was lumbered with the job of arranging the programme. I also had to provide most of the demonstrations and write to various lecturers for their help, apart from giving a large slab of the lectures myself. I gulped slightly when I realized the date fixed for the conference—the very date our third child was due. It would have to be broken to Clare gently. I just hoped everything would work out in the end.

Organizing the conference was a tremendous challenge. There was not only all the administration—but also the preparation of the field work. With two weeks to go, I decided to walk round the estate. I hadn't got very far when, to my horror, I found a whole conservation area under threat. The farmer of the land next to the College estate had agreed to let us use one of his species-rich wetland pastures for a demonstration. Now I found him busy getting his tractor hitched up to a fertilizer-spreader. The field was showing a fine flush of spring plants and flowers, lady's smock, celandines, buttercups and a few rare cowslips. I thanked my lucky stars that I was on very good terms with Fred Bloomfield. I could hear him starting his engine so I broke into a run across his field.

'Fred! Fred! I say, hold it a minute,' I shouted.

As I came up to him I said, between gasps, 'Fred, you know you agreed that we could bring the conference bunch here to show 'em your beautiful bit of wet pasture land?' He nodded. I continued, 'If you spread fertilizer all over the plants, it will destroy them. As a special favour, could you hold off this area of the field at least until after the conference—please?'

He pushed his battered old hat back on his head and sat there on the tractor while he pondered the matter. I knew it was asking a great deal. It could mean upsetting all his farming schedule. At that moment something made me glance beyond his tractor into short grass a metre or two ahead of the offside front wheel. I could hardly believe

74

it—there, beautifully camouflaged, was a nest which I was pretty sure was a lapwing's. Indeed, I had seen a pair wheeling and twisting over that bit of land some days ago. I walked quickly past Fred as he sat on, no doubt wondering what I was up to, and peered down at the nest. Sure enough, there were four dark, creamy-buff eggs with brown spots and blotches all over. They were indeed a lapwing's.

I straightened up and beckoned to Fred.

'Take a look at this, Fred.'

He got down stiffly and came and stared at the nest. His eyes widened.

'Well, an't that jest extr'ord'nry! Cor! If I'd started up I'd've jest smashed the lot. What are they, Peter?'

'Peewits.'

'OK, I'll leave this bit of the field. I suppose it won't make all that much difference with the work in the long run.'

'Thanks, Fred. I'm much obliged.'

Modesty should forbid, but I must say that the Wetlands Conference went off very well. It lasted three days. On day two we had a conducted tour of Fred's field, taking in a survey of the flora and fauna. There was a wonderful variety of birds feeding—snipe, wagtails, a rare green sandpiper—also an early orange-tip butterfly, frogs and even a very large grass snake basking amongst rushes. The flora study revealed jointed sedge and early spotted marsh orchids. We were especially careful to give the lapwing's nest a wide berth, but, even so, the bird took off with its crazy flight across the field and its plaintive 'Peewit'.

I got back home at the end of each day thoroughly exhausted. Though I enjoyed speaking about my special subject—wildlife management of ponds—the several sessions a day were keeping me on my toes. Constant questions from people who often had greater academic qualifications than my own, but less experience on the ground, were stimulating but exhausting. Anyway, you can only stand on your toes for limited periods.

It was tough on Clare too, looking after the two children all day expecting the third any moment. She really needed all the help I could give her at home. Anyway, we were hoping we could just get through the conference before anything happened. One comfort was that the College and the hospital were next-door neighbours.

And so we ended the second day, with the last day of the conference the next day. It just had to happen! That night Clare went into labour. We hung on until the morning and then I took her into hospital. We had barely got her settled before the contractions started.

I stood outside the delivery room while she was being examined by the houseman. He came out wagging his head. 'She's going to be some hours yet. You can go home and have your breakfast. We'll call you.'

I had made it clear that I would like to be present at the birth. Before I left, I told the sister that I'd got to give a lecture that morning at the College. But I had had a brilliant idea. The lecture was to be given in a building just across a field from the hospital and the delivery room window was visible from the lecture theatre. Could she just possibly give me the word that the baby was nearly there by waving a towel at the window—I'd be over in a couple of minutes? She smiled and promised to wave the flag.

I tore off home, snatched a toast-and-marmalade sandwich, entrusted the two children to the care of our kind next-door neighbour and drove off to College. The lecture was called 'Creating Ponds for Wildlife'. How I got through it I don't know, what with trying to keep one eye on the window, one on the hundred conference members, and another on my notes! They must have thought I'd got some strange nervous tic which made me jerk my head towards the window. Suddenly, the towel waved! I had only a few more sentences to deliver but I cut it to one. Gabbling out, 'Sorry, I'll have to go. Could we have questions during the afternoon session?' I dashed for the door.

The audience probably thought I'd been taken short. I ran like a hare across the field, into the hospital and up to the delivery room. Clare turned her face towards me and gave me a smile. Then her face screwed up into an expression of grim endurance.

'You just made it,' whispered the houseman to me.

I stood by Clare and held her hand. Her slender hands are well kept and soft in spite of the ravages of washing up. But, as her lips tightened again, she gripped my hand like a vice, until my fingers ached.

'P-u-u-sh!' urged the midwife, beginning to sound like someone with a stomach-ache of her own.

'What do you think I'm blooming well doing?' muttered Clare.

'P-u-u-u-sh! P-u-u-u-sh!' I could just see the top of the baby's head appearing, covered in smeary dark hair and with the face downwards.

'P-U-U-SH! P-u-s-h, push—all right, STOP pushing. Now brea-eathe, breathe, breathe, fine!'

The midwife was gently easing the baby's head out. Its small red features were all squashed and still. Skilfully she plucked out one tiny arm and shoulder, then the other, and then, lifting the baby upwards, she drew out the whole of his little body. Finally, we heard that indescribably welcome sound, the first explosive, rasping, half-choked, cry of protest of the newborn announcing his arrival in this harsh, inhospitable world. That little exasperated voice gave such obvious relief and satisfaction to them all. As for me I felt like kissing them all, except the houseman. But I wanted to shake his hand too.

Clare heaved a great sigh, screwed her head to one side to get a look at the baby who was now having his cord tied and cut off, and grinned with a look of pleasure and achievement. I gave a sigh of relief. All the way through, I had involuntarily been straining and relaxing in time with Clare until I felt quite in need of a rest myself.

'You did well, Mrs Hamilton,' said the houseman.

'I've had a bit of practice,' said Clare weakly but with a touch of her normal dry humour.

'Here, grab hold of your new son,' said the sister, passing me the bundle. He was all wrapped up, apart from a pouting little face, just like a parcel. 'Give him to your wife to cuddle while we get things shipshape.'

Clare stretched up a pair of tired hands eagerly to take him. 'Hullo Tommy,' she whispered. We had already decided on 'Thomas' if he were a boy. I bent over her.

'Darling, I'll have to go back to the conference but I'll come and see you tonight. Isn't he super! Thank God.' She managed to give me a brief kiss. And so I left her, literally holding the baby.

I snatched a meat pie and a cup of coffee in the College cafeteria. Sitting by myself at a table in an alcove, I tried desperately to compose my thoughts for the closing afternoon session which was to be followed by a question time. I took a grip on myself and in spite of everything the lecture went quite well. Fortunately, it was one of my favourite subjects—fresh water ecology.

After the lecture and the customary 'Any questions?' I sat down and waited in the inevitable silence while someone plucked up courage to take the plunge. Then a nice-looking young farmer, who had come all the way from the Cambridge fen country, rose to his feet. I waited, revolving in my mind possible opening gambits.

'I have a question which has been asked by the majority of those present. Will Mr Hamilton kindly tell us the name of his new baby?'

There was a burst of suppressed laughter from the audience, followed by a short round of applause. I grinned. Someone had spilt the beans. For my money it was Bill's wife, who was a ward cleaner at the hospital. I would fix it with Bill afterwards!

'He is to be called Thomas,' I said. The questioner bowed and the applause broke out again. I was quite touched at their interest.

When they had all settled down, serious questions came thick and fast, some for other lecturers and some for me. After tea, and a number of handshakes and congratulations, the whole mob moved out to the car park and began their exodus in cars and Land Rovers. Before he climbed into his Volvo Estate, the young Cambridgeshire farmer shook me by the hand and quietly handed me an envelope. I thanked him and waved him off.

When I got into the office where the faithful Daisy was doing some (unpaid) overtime in clearing up, I opened the envelope. Inside was a birth card with a lovely reproduction of a farm scene on the front, and inside: '- Congratulations to Mr and Mrs Hamilton on the safe arrival of their new son. May we respectfully suggest that his full name be Thomas Wetlands Hamilton.' With the card were two ten-pound notes.

After the conference I had three days' compassionate leave to look after Clare and the household. Having had a normal delivery, Clare was discharged after the statutory two days, to the care of the district midwife. Initial difficulty with breast-feeding was soon over and the baby settled down so that we got a fair amount of sleep at night (or at least an hour here and there).

It wasn't long before I was back in the office as usual, catching up with the backlog of letters, reports, figures on egg production, bills, requests from schools for Farm School visits and all the daily business of the Centre. Suddenly there was knock on the door and in came Bill Henman.

'Boss, would you come down to the poultry unit. Fred Bloomfield's got something for you.' I heaved a sigh, for I had a great deal of work to do, and followed him. What did Fred want? The conference visit to his wetlands pasture had been a huge success.

'Hullo, Fred,' I said as cordially as I could, 'what can I do for you? Thanks, by the way, for letting us come on your land. I hope we didn't do too much harm. Must have looked as if a herd of elephants had gone through.'

He smiled, 'I brought this.' He held out a small cardboard box. I opened it. Inside, wrapped up in cotton wool, were four lapwing eggs. I looked up at him.

'Fred,' I said, and my voice was disapproving, 'you didn't disturb the mother after all?'

He looked at me rather reproachfully. 'Course I didn't, Peter. I'm sorry, but it was after you brought the conference crowd round. Bird took off and she didn't come back. After several hours I knew she'd deserted, so I took a box down, put the eggs in the cotton wool and kept 'em in the kitchen by the Aga. I thought, though, you'd better have 'em in your incubator. An' if they hatch, perhaps you'd care for the chicks, for I jest an't got the time, nor the knowhow.'

I was filled with remorse for having misjudged him. 'Sorry, Fred, I might have known you'd not treat the birds badly. And thanks, we'll do our best, but I don't know—after a night without the mother's sitting . . .'

'It was a pretty warm night, Peter, but we'll jest have to see.'

It was a week later when I arrived in the morning that Bill reported the first fledgling had hatched. Soon two more followed but the fourth never did.

Bill seemed fascinated by the little balls of fluff. He never grumbled at having to add to all his other chores by collecting grubs and, later, worms to feed them on.

When they were fully fledged, we took the box up to their field and carefully put it in tall marshy vegetation which would protect them against magpies and crows. Then we released them to fend for themselves.

Considering they were born about the same time as Tommy, we might well have saddled him with, 'Thomas *Peewit* Hamilton'.

13
Pigs in the Pews

I expect by now you have formed the impression that
there is never a dull moment in our lives. Fanatical
though I am about the environment, there is another all-
consuming aspect of my life. Have you ever wondered
why your parents gave you your particular name? Well—
it might have been Grandma's or Grandad's, or, say, a
that of famous sportsman whose success they hope you
will emulate. My parents called me 'Peter' after the
apostle, because they hoped I'd grow up to be a friend of
Jesus and try to share my faith in him with other people,
just as Peter did.

I hope it's worked out a bit that way. For years Clare
and I helped run a Youth Group, and took the young
people away each year to camp in Wales. What with
teaching them what it means to be a Christian and
occasionally speaking in our church or leading a student
group, I had got used to being in the limelight. So it
wasn't too great a shock when a local vicar sent an urgent
request for me to give a talk to young people from his
church.

So, here I was, sitting facing them over a thickly-
draped table, a typical church youth group. They were
fourteen- to sixteen-year-olds, about thirty of them in all.
They were cheerful, rowdy, ready to pick up instantly
any peculiarity about the guest speaker and not above

commenting in stage whispers, 'Boring!'

The group leader who introduced me was one of the old school, unfortunately. He was totally devoted to the kids, slaving away each week, quite voluntarily, to give them a good time at these youth nights: games first—table tennis, snooker and so on—and then the 'epilogue'. I was the 'epilogue'. I used the word 'unfortunately' about the leader because his introduction could hardly have been one more calculated to put the young people off me.

'Now, boys and girls, we have Mr Hamilton as our speaker tonight. He is a lecturer at an Agricultural College. I know you'll be interested in what he has to tell you—Mr Hamilton.'

With a start like that something dramatic was needed to save the meeting from total disaster. If I didn't grab them straight away I might just as well pack up and go home. But I reckoned I had something very worthwhile to communicate, even on a hot Friday evening. Besides I'd got a wonderful example in Jesus himself. He 'grabbed' his audiences, used to heavy religious discourses from the rabbis, with his stories of crooked vineyard managers, angry householders whose beauty sleep was disturbed, drop-out sons and wandering sheep. So, though these were town kids, I'd got a few things from the country that even they would recognize.

'How many of you like boiled eggs?' A forest of hands shot up and there were a few disgusted 'Urghs' as well.

'Watch this.' I took a hen's egg from my pocket, put it on the table and gave it a push. As it rolled off I caught it neatly, to the evident disappointment of the audience who'd been hoping for a nice smash on the floor.

'Now, watch this.' I took a guillemot's egg, roughly the same size as the first, out of another pocket, put it on the table and gave it a push. It simply spun round and round on its axis like a top, being very narrow and pointed at one end.

'This is a guillemot's egg. The guillemot is a sea bird which lays its eggs on rocky ledges on cliffs. Now, if the guillemot leaves the ledge and flies off and the wind blows, the egg doesn't roll off the ledge and get smashed on the beach below. Because of its shape, the egg spins. Isn't that marvellous? I think God planned it that way.

'Now, you know it takes both a woman and a man to have children. Well, it takes a cock *and* a hen to have chicks. Even though a hen can lay eggs without a cock, those eggs won't produce chickens. So cocks are important. Like this one.'

I bent down behind the table and lifted out a handsome cockerel, letting him cling on to my wrist with his claws. By now the kids were hooked. They stared, open-mouthed. What was going to appear next?

I had already asked two of the group to help me. Now I continued, 'Do you remember a story from the Bible about a cock crowing? Kevin's going to read about it now.'

He read from Luke's Gospel: 'They arrested Jesus and took him away into the house of the High Priest; and Peter followed at a distance. A fire had been lit in the centre of the courtyard, and Peter joined those who were sitting round it. When one of the servant girls saw him sitting there at the fire, she looked straight at him and said, "This man too was with Jesus!"

'But Peter denied it, "Woman, I don't even know him!"

'After a little while a man noticed Peter and said, "You are one of them too!"

'But Peter answered, "Man, I am *not*!"

'And about an hour later another man insisted strongly, "There isn't any doubt that this man was with Jesus, because he also is a Galilean!"

'But Peter answered, "Man, I don't know what you are talking about!"

'At once, while he was still speaking, a cock crowed.

The Lord turned round and looked straight at Peter, and Peter remembered that the Lord had said to him, "Before the cock crows tonight, you will say three times that you don't know me." Peter went out and wept bitterly.'

At this point I held up the cock a little higher in front of the audience. 'You remember the story? Jesus had warned Peter that before the cock crowed Peter would say, three times, that he didn't know him.'

It was most extraordinary but, as I was speaking, I felt the cock's grip on my wrist tighten. He stretched up his neck and threw his attractive head back, opened his beak, and out came a perfect 'Cock-a-doodle-do!' If I had planned it, I couldn't have timed it better.

For a second the kids stared, then they burst into a perfect gale of laughter. I joined in.

'Yes, just like that,' I said when the laughter died down.

Then, obviously pleased by his audience's response, he crowed again. When the noise stopped I said, 'Now you won't forget that story! But why did the cock crowing matter so much to Peter? Because he knew that three times he had shied off letting people know he was a follower of Jesus. He was scared. Are you scared other kids at school will know you follow Jesus? Suppose someone said, "You're a Christian, aren't you?" What would you say?

'But perhaps you aren't a Christian, perhaps you're not following Jesus. Apart from this youth group, are you keeping well away from him? Following at a distance, like Peter? I've got a reminder about that too.'

From a larger crate under the table I lifted out a little piglet. Nice and warm in his straw, he'd been asleep and didn't like being woken up and hauled around, so I had to hold him tight. Thank goodness, he didn't do a job down my jacket, which piglets sometimes do if they get panicky. But he settled down.

'Now, how on earth does a pig make us think of

keeping well away from Jesus? Tricia's going to show us.'

Like Kevin, she'd been primed—this time to read from the Gospel of Luke about the prodigal son, who had left his father and his home and gone 'into a far country'. He had taken his inheritance too, but spent all his money in fast living, so he had to take a job feeding pigs. He got so hungry he felt like eating the pigs' food. He looked at the pigs and decided to go home to his father, say he was sorry and ask to be taken on as a servant. But his father spotted him coming and gave him a terrific welcome, new clothes and a party to celebrate his coming home.

'"That's what God is like," Jesus was saying. So, when you see a pig like this little fellow, even when you have bacon for breakfast, ask yourself whether you want to be friends with God, or stay away.

'I haven't finished yet!' I said and bent down again to open the last crate, after putting the piglet back in his. I lifted out a half-grown lamb. By this time the audience was absolutely agog, waiting to see what was coming up next.

I signalled to the last reader, one of the bigger girls, and she read quietly but clearly from the first chapter of the Gospel of John, 'The next day John saw Jesus coming to him and he said, "There is the Lamb of God who takes away the sin of the world!"'

This lamb was the *pièce de résistance* in my three-point talk. 'You see,' I went on, 'when the people of Israel knew they had done wrong things, and had turned away from God, they used to sacrifice a lamb. When they did this God said he would forgive them and they could come close to him again. The lamb which was sacrificed was a 'picture' of Jesus. Because it is only through Jesus we can come close to God again. As John said, Jesus came to take away everyone's sin, by dying for them on the cross.

'So, when you see a cock, or hear one, ask yourself whether you're still far away from Jesus; when you see a pig, come back to God; and when you see a lamb, re-member Jesus died for you.'

That was the end of my message. It's amazing how animals can liven things up. I looked at the group. There had certainly never been an epilogue like this before.

'If you'd like to, you can come and take turns to stroke the animals. They won't mind, they rather like being made a fuss of!' I said.

Immediately there was a rush of eager animal-lovers. It was as much as Bob, the leader, and I could do to maintain order. They all wanted to be first to stroke the animals in their crates.

Having tea with Bob and his wife afterwards, he dropped his formal air. While his wife plied me with food, he beamed at me. 'That was great, Peter! If I'd given them one of my neat, three-point talks, it would have gone in one ear and out of the other. But they won't forget your live illustrations in a month of Sundays!'

I went home in the car, surrounded by my crates, feeling like a dog with two tails.

14

Froggy Went A-Courtin'

Spring 1977 could be termed the spring of the frogs. By now baby Tommy was growing fast, behaving as *I* feel a baby should. He was placid, taking avidly whatever nourishment was placed in his mouth, and sleeping soundly throughout the night. Our one concern was his steadfast disinclination to assume the posture of *Homo erectus*. He preferred to remain *Homo sedentarius*, from which position his cherubic countenance gazed benignly on his little world.

Now I felt more free to undertake journeys to distant parts in order to take part in conferences and demonstrations. The one that sticks in my mind took place in a sumptuous hotel near Maidstone. I was billed to speak to an assembly of Kentish farmers on 'Pond development for conservation of wildlife and for profit'.

Always keen on visual aids, to remind my audience what an amphibian was and to allow them to see the increasingly rare common frog, I had brought with me a fine specimen, housed securely in comfortable travelling quarters. I found to my disappointment that there was a certain lukewarmness about these hard-headed and increasingly hard-pressed farmers. Many of their ponds were either overgrown, fouled by fertilizer or effluent, or filled in to provide a small increase in pasture acreage. They seemed indifferent to the fate of the common frog.

Speaking immediately after a good lunch, both solid and liquid, I found it hard to stir them for the first ten minutes.

It was providential that this was the moment that the frog decided to see what was going on. He leapt, without warning, from his box and, with one stupendous effort, landed in the front row of the audience. Trying rather unsuccessfully to restrain my mirth, I retrieved him.

At this point the audience sat up, began to listen and, even leant forward as I produced figures which I had got from my friend, Jack Easebourne. His figures showed that, by stocking with rainbow trout and letting the fishing rights, he had speedily recovered the cost of re-excavation of his pond and was beginning to make money out of it. I even raised a roar of laughter with my story of the plastic heron that had put me in my place.

With some trepidation I gave the reason for my concern for conservation as primarily the desire to care of God's creation. There was quite an enthusiastic round of applause when I sat down.

There were several more lectures, including one from a Sussex farmer who had got a flying start which predated the later 'set-aside' policy. (This was the plan in the 1980s to stop surplus Common Market food production by rewarding farmers who 'set aside' land from cultivation to rest it or grow hay or trees.) This particular farmer had planted woodlands, and, three years later, he was getting a fair return from his plantations of mixed woodland. He was selling firewood from his thinnings and finding custom from hurdle-makers who wanted his coppiced young chestnut trees.

At the end, several farmers came up, anxious to talk over rehabilitating their ponds. One shook me warmly by the hand and thanked me for my honesty in giving my basic concern.

'I'm a Christian too and that's how I feel,' he said.

I finally left Maidstone by car late in the afternoon, my

mind full of frogs and fish. I made good time up the motorway and eventually found myself coasting along our country lane, nearly back to our house, with headlights on.

Suddenly the beam picked out an amazing sight. Twenty metres ahead there was literally an army of frogs crossing the road. This was nature run riot. We had an untouched field pond just over the hedge not far from our home. These frogs must have been on a mating march there, oblivious of its suicidal nature, for ours is a busy lane at almost any time.

I could see the lights of our living room a few metres further on, so I let out a stentorian cry for help. In a moment Clare appeared.

'What on earth's the matter?' she asked, just as she became aware that her feet were paddling in a sea of frogs. I suppose it's because she's hardened by years of being married to me and being required to handle all sorts of small creatures at my behest that she didn't flinch or retreat screaming.

'Darling, you must help, these frogs are going to be run over any minute. Have you got anything handy we could put them in?'

It wasn't exactly an intelligent question but instantly she seized the hem of her long, full skirt and held it out in the shape of a hammock.

'How about this?'

'Great!' I cried and began ladling frogs into it with both hands, keeping watch all the time for headlights of approaching cars.

'Dump 'em in the pond, love, will you?'

We were just by the open gate into the field and the pond was a mere ten metres away by the hedge. I could hear protracted splashing and then Clare was back with outspread skirt for another load. We got two more into the pond before some irate tooting from a car behind us compelled me to pull my car to the side, wheels half in the ditch, and watch sadly as a number of frog stragglers were flattened into pulp on the road.

'Darling, that was great, thanks a lot.'

'Think nothing of it,' she replied, 'you're the one who'll have to pay to get my skirt cleaned.'

Before I rode off to College next morning I took a quick look at the pond. The obstinate, ungrateful beggars! There wasn't a frog to be seen! We must have picked the wrong mating site. Fond as I am of frogs, it was quite a relief to return to my more appreciative and warm-blooded hens.

15

The Hamilton Menagerie

'Jackie, go and wash your hands at once.' Clare looked up from the end of the table where she was pouring out the tea.

'Oh Mum, do I have to? They're quite clean.'

'You've been handling that pigeon in your room, so, go—and—wash—your—hands!' Jackie gave up and went out to the downstairs cloakroom. We heard the water running.

'And don't run away all the hot water,' Clare called. The rushing noise stopped.

As she passed my cup she said, 'I do wish you hadn't let him have that bird in his bedroom, I'm sure it's not hygienic. He often leaves it out of its cage and it does its droppings all over the carpet.'

I drank my tea and maintained a strategic silence. Percy, as we called him, was a pathetic homing pigeon who had lost his way in a storm and landed in the chicken run, exhausted and with half his feathers missing. For some inexplicable reason, he had no leg ring to tell us his ownership. He needed to belong to someone, and Jackie was the obvious step-father, hence Percy's presence in his bedroom.

Percy wasn't the only waif or stray to be taken in. Over the years our house had become a haven for lost creatures. Not all were 'lost'. Some were simply outcasts, but I could never bear not to take them in and the house contained an ever-changing menagerie.

For instance, there was Bertram. He was a huge, indeterminately-coloured cat. One day I had been driving home along our lane. Ahead of me at the side of the road I spotted a large plastic bag which wriggled. Intrigued by this unusual sight, I stopped and picked it up. The bag was heavy and writhing but fortunately for the occupant it wasn't tightly tied up, or else suffocation, no doubt intended, would have finished the creature off. Warned by the row coming from the bag, I decided not to open it just then but waited until I was at home in the greenhouse. I cut the string and out came Bertram. He leapt from bag to staging and from staging to upper storage shelf and glared down at me, hissing, spitting and growling. He looked like a miniature sabre-toothed tiger. His long upper canines protruded over his lower lip; he was skin and bone and his coat was scraggy. Shutting the door, I went to get him some food and water. When I returned the cat was still on the shelf, so I stuck the dishes in and closed the door.

It took a week before Bertram became at all amenable, and by then he was looking a different cat. We still kept him strictly apart from our little black-and-tan mongrel terrier, Twinkle, but we let them eye each other through the glass. Before long they were on speaking terms and would jointly occupy the hearthrug quite amicably. Bertram lacked one privilege, however. He was not allowed upstairs. He had once got into my bed and shot to the bottom under the bedclothes, before I could hoof him out. I was in deadly terror of those fangs and had to strip the bed to remove him.

As time went by Bertram developed quite endearing behaviour. He was never so happy as when he lay on my chest with his paws round my neck, asleep, as we sat before the fire. He became a properly domesticated cat. Of course, we had our small flock of laying hens, but

Bertram was under strict orders never to enter the hen-run, on pain of a sousing with water. We felt a comfortable sense of a job well done with Bertram, until the fatal day.

'Dad, oh Dad!' The wail came from upstairs. I sprang up the stairs three at a time. Jackie was on his knees beside his bed, tears trickling down his cheeks. I bent down and looked underneath. There was a scattering of pigeon feathers over the carpet and to one end a sad little head was lying, its eyes closed. Percy had flown his last flight.

'Bertram!' I shouted in a voice of thunder as I raced down the stairs again. Bertram came sidling in from the back yard, a complacent look on his face and his tummy hanging down from overloading. One tell-tale fluffy feather hung from the fur of his throat.

Bertram was banished from the fireside for a week and every time we met I accused him in harsh tones of being a particularly foul brand of pigeon-fancier. Meanwhile Jackie was grieving for poor, deceased Percy. I decided something had to be done for Jackie. On the following Saturday we went into Bentwich market and bought him a young, bright-blue budgie, plus cage, from a stall.

But Bertram wasn't the only creature I found in the road. I think I have inherited particularly sharp eyesight. When I was a kid, I could always see wild things before my dad, though not before Mum. *She* would often point them out to me. Perhaps this is partly why I spot things on the road now. Whatever the reason, late one night only three months after the demise of Percy, the demotion (temporary) of Bertram and the arrival of Archie, the budgie, I spotted the most extraordinary object, right in the middle of a normally busy road.

The headlights shone on a small white shape, sitting there erect, looking for all the world just like a little china salt shaker. I stopped, walked cautiously towards it, and there, meticulously grooming its ears and whiskers, was —a white mouse! He made no protest as I carefully picked him up by the tail. As I did so, I saw, in the white glare of the headlights, that 'he' was really a 'her'. Her little teats were very visible and her shape showed that the time was nigh.

Despite giving me her usual despairing look, Clare found the mouse one of our cosy little boxes, lined it with pieces of paper, and Maisie the mouse (instantly so named) was housed. Soon we heard the unmistakable sound of tearing. I appointed Janie as assistant mouse-minder. When she opened the well-perforated lid later to take a supervised peep, she found Maisie comfortably ensconced in a heap of torn-up paper, quite at home.

A few days later, Maisie became very bashful. She only poked her nose cautiously through the little hole at the side of the box and hurriedly scoffed the bits of bread, corn grains and scraps when she thought no one was looking. I could see that her little tum was now very flabby. It was ten days before we dared open the box again. By this time the babies had a slight coat of fur. And now we had nine baby white mice to contend with.

It was then that we decided to do the only wise and, incidently, profitable thing. With his parents' permission and strict instructions to each purchaser, Jackie sold all the baby mice to his schoolmates at a reasonable price. Although Janie was temporarily heart-broken, she and Jackie enjoyed the proceeds of the mouse auction.

I have to confess I felt a considerable sense of relief to be shot of them, for it had become increasingly difficult to keep Bertram from showing too great an interest in our mouse population. Maisie remained alone to rule her fifty by twenty-five centimetre kingdom, with occasional outings up Jackie's sleeves or on Janie's lap. Fortunately Bertram, who had been showing increasing tendencies to revert to his primitive origins, had discovered the farm buildings across the field and became a welcome visitor and controller of the farmer's unwanted barn occupants.

Life is full of reverses. In an unguarded moment Jackie left the bedroom window open, while he cleaned out Archie's cage. In a flash Archie was out. He didn't even say 'goodbye', which he could have done, only "ello', as Jackie opened the cage door. Goodbye it was; and though Clare searched the fields, hedges and copses behind the house for days all she found a week later was a pathetic little pile of blue feathers underneath an oak where we knew a little owl roosted.

But there's nothing like a diversion to help a child stop moping. At that time I had just succeeded in hatching some ducklings from a wild mallard's eggs which we had found in a deserted nest on a College pond. So, to cheer everybody up, I brought home four of the ducklings and took them up to the children's bathroom. We cooled the water down until it was tepid. Janie and Jackie were in transports as the carefree little ducklings swam in and out between their legs (it is a very big bath), and dived like miniature submarines.

Then there were the lambs. The College shepherd, who must have heard somewhere that I was more or less nuts, offered me two lambs which were unable to walk. My long-suffering wife was dragooned into helping us bottle-feed them, and so Pegleg, who never got one back leg mobilized, and '42', so named from his ear-tag, became residents in their own enclosure in the rough grass at the end of the garden. The children loved them.

I am both a lover of animals and a realist. The children understood that lambs grow into sheep and sheep have one day to go off to become food, unless you are a vegetarian and then you don't keep farm animals anyway. But they found it hard. One day '42' went and did not come back. Sadly, Pegleg had an even shorter life. Mr Reynard got him early one evening just before dark. I had seen the fox skulking round and later I found Pegleg's feet, woolly skin and head in a ditch on the side of the farm lane.

16
Badgers and Bird-Brains

It could be said that I've always had a yen for badgers. I think it started when I was eleven or twelve. My first contact came way back in the spring of 1955 when one of Dad's colleagues invited the whole family to supper. After supper had been cleared away, Uncle Harry placed chairs in a semi-circle in front of the big french windows opening on to the garden and put out the light. It was already dark so he switched on a small light, illuminating the patio outside, and pulled back the curtains. We all took our seats expectantly.

A trail of raisins and small pieces of bread had been laid, leading up the lawn and ending on the patio immediately outside the window. We sat silently for about five minutes and then some small ghostly shapes appeared at the bottom of the garden. They advanced in fits and starts towards the window.

Before long, we could see three badgers, two larger and one smaller, probably a male, his mate and one offspring. As we watched, spellbound, we could see that they were eating the bait, but daintily and selectively, raisins being picked out and the bread left alone. They looked very healthy. They had narrow muzzles, black-and-white striped heads, grey-brown bodies, and short legs. They walked with a sort of scurrying waddle.

Making sure they hadn't missed a single raisin on the

way, they came right up to the window.

'Greedy pigs,' whispered Uncle Harry, 'leaving the bread as usual and going for the raisins!'

If the glass had not been there I could have stretched out my hand and touched them. When there was a slight altercation between a big one and the baby, I saw it was just as well I couldn't—a set of gleaming, sharp teeth flashed in the light. Then at an unguarded moment my little brother Barney, who was only six, escaped Dad's restraining grasp and advanced to press his nose to the window for a front-seat view. In an instant the badgers were in flight. They sped across the lawn and disappeared into the undergrowth beyond.

''Fraid the show's over for the evening,' said Uncle Harry, pulling the curtains and switching on the light. 'They might come back later to clean up the bread, but we'll all be in our beds by then.'

I swallowed my irritation with Barney. After all, he was just a kid. As we were putting our coats on in the hall, I said, 'Thanks, Uncle Harry, that was terrific. How did you train them to come like that?'

'Well, I first saw them one night when I came in late from a call. I tried for a long time to entice them with different bits of food, until I hit upon raisins. They love 'em! But if they're hungry enough they'll come for bread now. They eat almost anything—especially worms. You should have seen the mess they made of our back lawn when we first laid turves! Came one night and threw the turves all over the place, rooting out worms with their noses! Still, we can put up with it just to see them. Glad you enjoyed it. Come and watch again one night, if you want to.' I did.

It was a year or two later when I watched badgers from the fork of a tree, and saw a bit more of their domestic habits. I began to make a collection of the footprints of wild creatures, pouring in liquid plaster of Paris and making casts. I recorded those of a fox, a rabbit, several larger birds and even a grey squirrel, and swore one footprint, found in a wood a mile or two in the country behind Wilverton, was that of a pinemarten. Even the footprint of an iguanodon—a huge, two legged, three-toed dinosaur—was added to my collection when lime-stone foot casts were found in mudstone exposed by very high tides at Bexhill-on-Sea. But the oddest footprint in the collection at the time was that of a six-toed badger. The funny thing was that we had a six-toed cat... but it was just a coincidence.

We had several badger setts in various dry banks around the College farm. From fresh claw marks, freshly dug earth and wisps of gathered grass, we knew that all were inhabited, and badger-watching became a regular feature of our wildlife courses for adults and sixth-formers. Instruction sheets sent out beforehand stated, 'Please wear inconspicuous clothes and when in the vicinity of the badger setts maintain quiet, and move as little as possible.'

One of the adult visits is engraved on my memory. I got home very late that evening and was sitting at our kitchen table, with a soothing mug of coffee, while I told dear Clare the full story.

'We had twenty adults altogether. I don't want to sound prejudiced but I had my suspicions of Eustace Barkworth right from the start. He was much younger than the others, about nineteen and as cocky as they come. I could see we were in for trouble. In spite of my warnings on the instruction sheet, he showed up wearing a brilliant-red anorak and a long white scarf with tassels. On the way over the fields he smoked a cigarette and I could hear him telling a girl who was probably the next youngest, in her twenties, how he knew a lot about badgers.

'"Watched 'em often on my dad's farm. I reckon there's not much to 'em, probably covered in fleas, an' you know, they reckoned down in the West Country that they could carry TB to the cattle. The farmers shot a lot a while back, my dad says. Don't know why I bother comin' on a show like this. Good thing to add to my notes, I suppose; I'm doing a one-year agricultural diploma course before I start work on our farm.''

'When we were about fifty metres away from the sett and it was getting dark, I stopped and asked them all to keep quiet and move carefully. Eustace shut up for a bit, but then I could hear him whispering on about himself and his badger knowledge again. When we were about ten metres from the sett we all stopped and sat down. After about a twenty-minute wait we heard a scraping noise and a large female came backwards out of the hole dragging a bundle of used bedding after her. Shortly afterwards, a big male came out of the next hole, sat down and began scratching himself. Can you beat it? That was the moment our friend Eustace stood up with his blessed plastic anorak crackling like anything, to stretch his leg.

' "Got the bloomin' cramp," he said, only he didn't say 'blooming'. He said it in a loud whisper and the badger must have heard him. Do you know, the old brock just lifted his head and stared in our direction and then went back to his scratching. The sow did nothing except begin gathering dried grass.

'Eustace was facing the other way. He seemed so casual about the whole exercise that I began to doubt whether he'd been aware that the badgers had arrived at all. He rubbed his leg furiously, then looked on the ground and found the raised root of an oak tree. He sat down on it, with a few more crackles, and leant back against the tree and closed his eyes.'

I paused, took a swig of coffee and broke off a bit of digestive biscuit. As I leaned back in the chair, I very nearly closed my eyes. It had been a weary day and I was glad it was Saturday tomorrow and I would have a break from Eustaces and even badgers.

'You can't stop there,' said Clare. 'What happened after that?'

I roused myself, took another bit of biscuit, washed it down with coffee and went on. 'Sorry, this really was the best bit. We had a whole hour, and there were five badgers in the end. They went through their whole routine, cleaning the sett, putting in fresh bedding, little ones playing and pretending to fight, parental discipline and sharpening claws on a tree stump. Every now and then I noticed heavy breathing under the tree, and once the girl Eustace had been talking to had an attack of the giggles which she manfully suppressed. Then the badgers went off, probably to their feeding grounds around the farm or to dig up some unsuspecting person's lawn for worms. We all stood up and stretched our weary limbs. All except Eustace. The girl was giggling outright and she went over and shook his shoulder. He gave a snort and a grunt and sat up.

'He looked around him, and guess what he said: "Well, when does the show begin?"'

'A big hearty bloke with mutton-chop side-whiskers said, with a strong Welsh accent, "Sorry, but you've had it, bach!"'

'Eustace was livid. Said he hadn't come all that way just to sit on damp ground and he wanted his fees back. I had a word with him and pointed out that there had been a good evening's badger-watching and, anyway, the fees were chiefly for the very good meal they'd had in the College canteen and for the other parts of the course. He was still grumbling when he got into his hotted-up Ford Escort. Although he was such an idiot, I felt sorry for him.'

I shook my head and yawned. 'Time for bed,' I said. 'And it's Saturday tomorrow,' I added. 'We're off to the mountains. But first, we need some rest.'

I woke, as usual, at about six. Clare, as usual,

slumbered on. I simply lay there, thinking deep thoughts, an unusual luxury reserved for Saturday morning and the blessed relief from toil. Good old Bill would attend to the poultry. He would be there early—an hour or two twice a day would be enough for routine feeding and egg-collecting and grading. I remembered how we had told the children the night before that we would go for a trip into the mountains. A fifty-mile drive into Wales took us to a lovely quiet place where we had often been before.

There was something so special, so unspoilt, about the mountains. I still carried memories of the great forests and mountains of Kenya from my childhood. They had spoken to me of the greatness of God, and I wanted our children to have that inheritance too and to be able to thank him. They weren't too young to grasp just an inkling of their loving Father's creation and it would be at its best on this beautiful morning.

I could hear the two older children in their beds in one room telling each other stories and Tommy banging around in his cot in the room next door. Now Clare was awake. If we wanted peace for our morning prayer together we'd better have our tea smartish and get on with it. We had just finished our brief Bible reading and prayers before the children came in and Tommy began yelling to be plucked from his cot.

'Now what are we going to do today?' I asked them.

'Have a picnic in the mountins,' said Jackie.

'In the mountings,' echoed Janie.

'Well, let's ask Jesus to take us safely there. Hands together and close eyes.' Sitting in my dressing-gown at the end of the bed, I felt a little check in my throat to see them all in a row with Clare, and Tommy peeping through his fat little fingers at me.

'Thank you Jesus for a lovely new day. May we have a happy time in the mountains and be kind to each other.'

'Amen,' said everybody.

It took us about two hours to get into Wales and the

Berwyn mountains, to an unspoilt little village called Llanarmon where the main tributary of the Ceiriog river runs under a stone bridge on its way to cross the Llangollen canal and flow into the Dee. At Llanarmon the river is just a stream a few metres wide but there are lots of brown trout in it. It was a treat to see that crystal brook. So many of our local rivers were polluted. We didn't stop in Llanarmon but went on up the valley following a tiny one-track road running steadily higher and higher, the stream deep in the valley below. Passing a Methodist chapel, a heritage from the Welsh revival at the beginning of the century, we dropped a little and left the car beside the road near a stone-built farm. We took to a path on foot, with Tommy in a rucksack on my back.

We trudged on through the heather and at last we were looking down at our goal, a small patch of mountain grass beside a pool at the foot of a waterfall. I had a plunge in the icy water before lunch but couldn't persuade any of the others to join me. We had a wonderful afternoon, lazing and watching trout with Jackie and Janie.

The only other human beings we saw were an elderly gentleman and his wife who came down the stony track through the pass above, wheeling bicycles. I just *had* to climb up from the river to the path and have a word with them after they stopped and looked down at us. He was a retired primary-school headteacher who was touring North Wales with his wife by bicycle and his special interest was birds! I envied him; he had actually watched choughs, ravens and a red kite higher up in the mountains behind. I looked forward to the time when the children were older, and could come with me on bird-watching expeditions.

As a small compensation I did see a pair of ring ouzels in some bushes on the other side of the stream. Then high overhead I saw two buzzards swinging in sweeping arcs. Suddenly they dropped on some prey in the heather high up on the round-topped mountain above us. Dear Clare, whose first interest is always keeping the children happy (she tolerates and even feigns an interest in my feathered friends to keep me happy), had played games with the children while I went bird-watching. She had tea from a thermos flask at the ready when I came back. Then we headed for home, stopping only to pick up some fish and chips on the way.

It was an idyllic weekend. After going to church on Sunday we had a peaceful walk round the fields at the back of the house and went to bed early.

On Monday, when I cycled into College, I felt ready for anything. As I pedalled down the last stretch to the College gates I saw something on the roadside. It was a full-grown female badger. She would never suckle her young again. She had been mangled by car wheels.

17

'Pons Asinorum'

Before I mounted my trusty (and rusty) bike that evening for my ride home, I went down to look at the College pond which I had rescued from obliteration early on in the conservation programme. I stood a few metres from the edge in the pleasant evening light. It had taken five years to get this far. It was beautifully established now with a small screen of growing trees: alder, gean and sallow. The pond had nice clean edges—not broken and trampled by the feet of cattle, which were kept out by a wire fence. A healthy bed of water plantain, reed mace and branched bur-reed grew round the margins, and there was a generous growth of water hornwort, to keep the water oxygenated. Insect life, too, was plentiful, with two or three species of damselfly and dragonfly. I got an occasional glimpse of frogs and three-spined sticklebacks and even a smooth newt.

As I cycled down the College drive, I noted that everything had been spruced up—the drive was weed-free with edges neatly cut and the lawns had been almost manicured. Some of the more hirsute students had even trimmed their beards. Why all this tidiness? Princess Anne was to pay us a visit on the morrow. Not to see my pond, but to open formally our new Food and Dairy Technology Department. The following day the programme was carried off with great gusto, not to say éclat.

But what I appreciated most was the way the Princess took a leaf out her dad's book and included in her speech, which was really very funny, a good strong plug for conservation in the farming programme; I was quite ashamed at the vigour of my applause.

A number of College courses were transferred to the fine new buildings and even I took a peep inside to see the gleaming stainless-steel apparatus from which finer food for the future would be produced. But that term most of my time would be taken up with the season's series of Farm Schools and visits to town primary and secondary schools. So it was that I had hardly noticed the trench in which the effluent pipe carrying dairy washings from the new unit lay.

The whole complex had been designed by a well-known local architect who specialized in the more technical farming structures and I had been confident that everything would be satisfactory from an environmental point of view. So it was a week at least before I found the time to carry out an inspection of the pond. To my horror, I found that the effluent pipe trench from the new unit, with its outlet valve for irrigation pipes, stopped just three metres away from the pond! I gave up my inspection, went quickly back to the College administrative office and asked to see the principal. His secretary left his door open and he shouted through, 'Come in, Peter.'

'Can you spare me a minute?' I asked, keeping my cool.

'How long is a minute?' he said with a smile. 'Sit down. What can I do for you?'

I sat down. I was well aware that my bull-at-the-gate reputation had not exactly endeared me to the principal, but I hoped I had now lived down my early brashness. We had a good working relationship.

'I'm sorry to bother you, but I've just been down to the demonstration pond. I've found that the effluent pipe from the new unit ends just three metres away. Will the dairy washings come out there into the field?'

His smile waned.

I went on, 'If so, there is bound to be seepage into the pond. With a high level of organic material in the washings, it's bound to pollute the water and cause de-oxygenation. So we might as well write the pond off as a demonstration resource for our schools' freshwater studies and a conservation site. Couldn't the pipe be extended to carry the effluent at least past the pond?'

I had the feeling that we might find ourselves back at square one, so I was ready to play my trump card about the schools' work straight away. The once despised and later tolerated schools' work had begun to prove quite a feature in the College prestige ratings. 'It will be a big setback for the schools' work,' I repeated.

The principal supported his chin on his left fist and fiddled with a paper-knife with his other hand.

'I see your point, but have you any idea of the cost of the effluent piping? To be effective, it would have to run into the main sewage and, at a conservative estimate, I'd say it would mean finding at least another three or four thousand pounds. Anyway, we don't know whether it will really cause any appreciable damage to your pond. After all, it's at least three metres away, as you say. I'm sorry, but I'm afraid it's out of the question.' I could see there was no point in prolonging the discussion, so I nodded and went out, to wait for the worst.

The worst didn't happen. The pond continued to flourish. I suspect that the principal had taken a quiet walk down there on the sly. At any rate, I thought there was a small gleam of satisfaction in his eye when we met. A pair of mallard had taken up residence in the reeds there and even brought up a troop of ducklings. My worries then were transferred to the possibility of Mr Reynard paying a visit one night. I visited the pond one evening in early summer. Brown *Aeshna* dragonflies and small blue damselflies hovered and mated above its clear, tranquil waters. I thought back to the overgrown, choked pond we had rescued five years ago.

The next day I was preparing for a school's visit. Studies on the pond-life were part of the work schedule. On my way down to the pond, I caught the whiff when I was still fifty metres away. It was like the smell of the cesspool down our garden at home. My heart sank. I stood once more on the edge. The water had gone a cloudy grey. By the following day plant life was beginning to die and by the next almost every visible bit of life in the pond had vanished. Small sticklebacks floated dead on the surface, bloated frogs were squirming on the verges; it was a total disaster.

I went back to the College and marched into the principal's office without ceremony.

'Mr Brazenhall, would you please come down and take a look at the pond?'

Without demurring he got up and we walked down in total silence. I think he had guessed what to expect. As he stood and looked at the ruin of what had been a really attractive little area of conservation, his face was a study. There was a mixture of regret and even consternation in it. He turned.

'Peter, what can I say? I am very sorry this has happened. I realize how disappointed you must be after your years of work on this project. First we must find out what went wrong, for, you must agree, things hadn't turned out as badly as you feared up until now. Then we'll really have to see what can be done about it.'

I didn't say anything. I really didn't know what I could say.

When it all came out, we found that a member of the farm staff had opened the outlet valve connected to the irrigation pipe and the equivalent of a few buckets of very potent dairy effluent had seeped into the pond. Mr Brazenhall promised to get the pond pumped out, but it was a bit late in the day. I realized that I had just got to start all over again and build up the pond-life from scratch. But there was one very considerable recompense. Mr Brazenhall got in touch with the authorities and squeezed the money out of them to pay for joining the effluent pipe to the main sewage from the College. It cost, he told me, more than four thousand pounds.

He called me into his office to tell me, giving me a friendly clap on the shoulder. 'I guess it would have been cheaper, Peter, if we'd done the job when you first brought it up,' he said generously.

I thanked him and went out. A new idea was already simmering in the old brain. In this atmosphere of good-will it might just come off. But, I must still pick my moment. I had been aware for some time of the growing conviction of conservationists that fertilizer contamination was doing harm to pond-life. Suppose I could create buffer zones about three metres wide of unfertilized grass around one or two ponds on the farm. Then I could prevent fertilizer seepage from spreading into the ponds. By doing this it should be possible to demonstrate a beneficial effect on pond-life. So my pond disaster could be the 'open sesame' to a new approach to this side of farming and conservation. I might even submit the research as part of an MSc thesis.

There had been so much on my mind that as I cycled home I felt ripe for a little light relief. I wondered what there would be on television—the usual drivel probably, but there might be a good nature film or something really funny. Clare had cooked one of her marvellous suppers, chicken pie and apple crumble. She insisted that I had my supper first before she let me look at the day's post. There were a lot of farming adverts and some rather loony conservation effusions but there was also a letter from Mum and Dad. We wrote back and forth every week. Dad said I just wrote off the top of my head (which was probably pretty accurate) but that they liked it that way.

Mum's writing was copperplate but Dad's needed a chemist to interpret—it was a typical doctor's writing.

What amused me tonight was the address at the top of their letter. 'Powerstock Railway Station, near Leominster.' I'd heard Dad tell the corny story of the lavatory attendant who was a bit dim. (He was found by the Charing Cross stationmaster camping out with his family outside the Gents because he'd been told he could have his holiday 'at his own convenience'.) But *this* seemed a bit much!

However, the letter explained it. Mum and Dad were taking a short break at a bed-and-breakfast place in a station house on a redundant railway. It was apparently a beautiful spot. Their bedroom looked down on the disused platform and growing along the old track were many beautiful and rare wild flowers, among which were some thorn-apples, described in botanical works, a plant with a prickly fruit *Datura stramonium*, often found in old sites newly disturbed. Looking up from the bedroom they had a full view of a tumulus, a prehistoric burial ground, on top of a three-hundred-foot hill. All this was a very welcome diversion from my College battles. So I put all my whirling thoughts about ponds, fertilizers and conservation to the back of my mind.

But the next day I decided to strike while the iron was hot. I brought up the subject of the ponds with the College principal. He looked at me quizzically.

'I can see you've got over your "*Ponds Asinorum*!"' he said, laughing. 'This new idea sounds a feasible project. I'll let you know in a day or two when I've had time to talk to the farm manager and College governors.'

I thought this seemed hopeful but I didn't quite like the sound of his '*ponds asinorum*'. My Latin only reached prep-school standard, and his words sounded like something slightly insulting. Rather than betray my ignorance, I looked it up in the dictionary we kept in the office. There wasn't a '*ponds asinorum*' only '*pons*'. I got the drift. In Latin *'pons asinorum'* literally means *'asses''* bridge. The dictionary told me it signified 'an impassable barrier to further progress', and also, 'a severe test for a beginner'. I could take my pick!

A few days later the principal let me know that I could carry on and create my buffer zones and that the managers would neither plough nor fertilize in the chosen area. I just couldn't wait to get started.

18
The Captain's Log

'You oughter go and see old Captain Forsyte. He'd tell you a thing or two about that meadow. Been 'ere donkey's years 'e 'as; took a real interest in it an' all.' Bill turned to fill the basket with the eggs from the nest boxes in the free-range section of the poultry unit. We were on our rounds. As I went on to the turkey section I thought about what he'd just said. But for the moment my attention was taken up with the turkeys.

These were no ordinary turkeys. We had taken on a flock of beautiful rare-breed turkeys from a turkey-breeding company to form a gene pool. Although this had meant extra work, especially for Bill, it had proved quite a windfall. Here was another subject to add to our programme of sixth-form studies. (Applied genetics was now part of the A level biology syllabus.) The value of the turkeys had also increased as primary schools bought the rare-breed eggs to incubate and hatch in school, producing young chicks (poults). In turn they were used in science and maths also and then the poults were given or sold to local City Farms, Farm Centres and to a Rare Breed Survival Centre. This made sure these rare breeds would be conserved.

I spared a thought for the poor old 'oven-ready' white turkeys. These have been bred with such bulging chests that they are unable to breed naturally. The next step down the hill will be reproduction by cloning. I mused on the fact that, although we can make identical cars cheaply which actually work, animals and birds kick back at mass-production. God didn't work that way in creation—he can see that each individual is different. God didn't create boring uniformity. I'm sure we shall pay for the way we treat animals.

The idea of a turkey-breeding company sounds rather unnatural, but the funny thing was that the turkeys came originally from an old farmer living in the west country. He had, single-handed, kept all the old breeds of turkey alive on his tiny farm. The company wisely bought him out.

Reluctantly I went back to the office to do some paperwork. The long-suffering Daisy and I spent the rest of the morning going over our annual report on the Aims and Plans of the Clampshire Outdoor Education Centre. When I read through her transcript I sighed and looked up at her.

'Daisy, I get bored just reading this. It's like a blooming catalogue.'

'Now look, Peter, that's only because you're so familiar with it all. Wait until you've filled in the details—that'll liven it up.' I thought about it. I remembered the looks on the faces of the children who had taken part. They hadn't found it boring. I remembered the teenager who came to a more advanced course and gave me an almost word-for-word account of what I had said on a Farm School visit to her primary school.

Our visitors ranged from inner-city children right up to hardened estate managers and experienced farmers. They all seemed to get a real kick out of their visits and came back for more. We weren't a play farm or a farm zoo. We could leave that to entrepreneurs or those who needed to diversify to keep out of bankruptcy.

That's not to say our funds weren't strictly limited. Indeed, they could hardly keep pace with our costs, but it is amazing how inventive one becomes.

I will not mention the location where I had one of my earlier 'make-do' inspirations. Light meters are very expensive but I found that looking through the cardboard tube from a used-up toilet roll is a simple method of measuring light penetration through the overhead leafage of a tree. You simply stand and gaze up at the leaves, make a fair estimate of the percentage cover, note it down, move back a metre and repeat the process until the edge of the tree is reached. Then count the number and species of plants on the ground within that area. This gives you the relationship between density of leaf cover and the variety and number of plants on the woodland floor. It may be rough, but I've checked it out and it's accurate enough.

The use of these homespun light meters did cause me some embarrassment when a tractor driver taking a short cut through the wood came across a posse of youngsters gazing heavenwards through a batch of toilet roll tubes. I think that convinced him that I really had finally gone round the bend.

It was just as well he didn't arrive on another day to find us measuring plant species in relation to soil compaction (solidity caused by pressure), or he would probably have called in a doctor on the spot. We were apparently nailing down the carpet of flowers to the woodland floor. Soil petrometers for measuring soil compaction are expensive. However, a very fair estimate can be obtained by using a fifteen-centimetre nail with marks filed at one-centimetre intervals. To get a fairly accurate result, the nail must be struck with a wooden mallet, using the same force and from the same height each time, into the woodland floor. The depth of penetration measured can be equated to the sort of vegetation capable of growing in that soil. The harder the soil, the harder the work for the plants.

We could have expended some of our hard-won funds

on oxygen meters to study oxygen concentration levels in water polluted by organic effluent. The better the oxygen levels, the greater the variety of animals in the water. But there are far cheaper and easier ways of measuring oxygen, using chemicals such as ferrous sulphate and methylene blue as an indicator. Also, the dramatic changes in colour were more interesting to children.

Perhaps the most successful and simplest idea was to look at the growth and structure of plants as indicators of nutrient levels. This meant there was no need for chemical analysis. I even used my own garden at home to demonstrate practical examples of wildlife management, using a miniature 'species-rich' meadow on our lawn near a small pond and a mixed-species hedgerow, all in about two hundred square metres. I doubt whether I would get a prize for a velvet lawn or a manicured hedge but that didn't worry me (though Clare sometimes moaned about my 'bringing my work home').

Anyway, that's all rather off the track. Back to my paperwork. I picked up the annual report again and set to work on the 'bare bones'. It needed it. At present it read:

Management of land for food production with protection of wildlife and the use of this as a learning resource.

Wildlife is our inheritance and the conservation of it is part of our responsibility.

Subjects for schools and college students.

Biology/Ecology—life cycles, breeding, genetics, food chains.
Geography—soils and land use.
Maths—animal growth rates, food conversions and percentage production.
Environmental Studies—pollution and the use of indicator plants and animals.

English—language development and essay writing.
Art—resources on a farm.
Creating wildlife habitats on school estates.

There were about ten more headings but these will give you the idea. It all looked so academic. But the Centre's work was such fun!

I was in the mood for a little light relief, and suddenly remembered old Forsyte. He might just be the bloke to give it. I'd had my eye for a long time on a small field in an awkward corner of the College farm which seemed beautifully neglected. Captain Forsyte's old country house and garden were next to it. I cycled round and turned up his drive. It was a cold day and he was indoors. As I went up the steps to the front door I saw him at the bay window of the front room looking out over the field with a pair of old binoculars. They were huge. They could have formerly been naval issue, probably Barr and Stroud. (I recognized them as Dad had bought me a pair when I was at school. Very heavy but with good magnification and very wide field.)

I rang the bell and an elderly housekeeper came to the door.

'Good afternoon. I'm Peter Hamilton and I am in charge of outdoor education at the College next door. I was wondering if I could have a word with Captain Forsyte.'

'Would you please wait in the hall while I go and ask him?' She was polite but one of the old school—job number one is to protect the master. She knocked at the door, went in, and I could hear a murmur of voices. Then the door opened and the captain himself came out.

'Come in, my boy, haven't I heard a bit about you, helping to protect our wildlife eh?' He seized my hand. 'Come in, come in. Sit down. Now what can I do for you?'

I sat down in an old leather armchair and he lowered

himself stiffly into another.

'Well sir, I have a particular interest in that meadow.' I pointed at it through the window. 'I think it looks wonderfully undisturbed and has probably got a lot of unusual plants and wildlife which I think should be conserved. And it could be, under careful supervision, a great teaching source for the schoolchildren I have on field courses too. I have been given to understand you have been interested in it for much longer than I have. I wondered whether you would tell me of any of your observations.'

He was a small man with white hair. Under his white eyebrows a most penetrating pair of blue eyes shone out, set in a weatherbeaten, lined face. He had one hand cupped round his left ear and as he listened his old face broke into a broad grin.

'Certainly, certainly, my boy. Now you come over to my desk and I'll show you something.' I got up and took the chair by his desk which he pointed to, while he dragged forward another one and sat beside me. He pulled open a wide drawer on the right-hand side of his desk and took out a well-bound volume like an account book. He opened it and I bent over to read it. It was wonderful! The first page was dated March 1956 and, just like a ship's log with dates, there, recorded in copperplate handwriting, were scores of wild plants, animals, birds and insects which he had meticulously noted. It was a naturalist's goldmine.

I scanned the entries, spellbound. Plants: tormentil; large burnet; field scabious; betony. Butterflies: small skipper; orange tip; pearl bordered fritillary. Birds: snipe; heron; water rail. Reverently I turned the pages. Some of the gaps between the dates were longer than others, but it was a unique recording of observations made in a circumscribed area. The last entry was made on the previous day, and, though the handwriting had become spidery, it was still as legible as print.

'Captain Forsyte, this is marvellous. How on earth did you find the time to do it all?'

He smiled with just a hint of pride, then he shrugged and said, quite quietly, 'Had a lot of time on my hands since my wife went on and, in spite of all my years at sea, I never lost my boyhood love of nature.'

His face lit up and he took my arm, 'Now I've seen some things in the navy which I'd guarantee you haven't, my boy! We stopped once outside the Galapagos and I had a boat put ashore and saw some marvels. Enormous giant tortoises, sea lizard, land iguana and many species of birds. I've never forgotten the experience.'

He was just like a schoolboy in his enthusiasm, and it rubbed off on me. I would have liked to have asked to borrow his records but I knew I shouldn't, as he was still recording. However, he did give me permission to call any day and take notes.

'Ye'll stay and drink a dish of tea with me, won't you?' He had a note of wistful appeal in his voice. 'It'd be good to have a talk with a real naturalist.'

I felt suddenly humbled. This elderly man, without any formal training, had painstakingly assembled data of real value and here he was calling me 'a real naturalist' because I'd had a bit of formal training and fifty times his opportunities. I knew I ought to get back and clear some work up at the Centre, but I couldn't be so churlish as to refuse his invitation.

'Thank you very much, I'd be delighted.'

'Good feller.' He got up, pressed a bell, and told the housekeeper to bring tea for two. Half an hour later I staggered out and mounted my bike, full of tea, salmon sandwiches, scones and jam and a slab of fruit cake that knocked spots off even the best that Clare ever baked. That housekeeper knew how to make a guest welcome!

19

Ponds and the Principal

Over the next few weeks I took advantage of Captain Forsyte's invitation and paid him several visits, carefully avoiding teatime. I got some amazing facts out of his records. Over the years our teams of schoolchildren had done surveys of the whole farm. The teachers and I had supervised them as they recorded birds, butterflies, wild flowers and grasses. On his own, from just that small meadow, the captain had recorded thirteen out of the sixteen species of butterfly and one hundred of all the varieties of wild flowers and grasses we had found. Armed with these facts I went to see the farm manager concerning any plans he might have for this bit of the College farm. It was vital to preserve this little natural treasure house without delay.

The farm manager didn't waste any words. He put down his cup of coffee, 'We're turning it into grassland: taking out that scrubby hedge that cuts it off, spraying it to get rid of the weeds, re-seeding with grass and moving the stock on to it when it's all shipshape.'

I was aghast. The thought occurred to me that if the old mariner Forsyte had heard him misuse that word 'shipshape' for what he proposed to do, he'd have had him clapped in irons. For a moment I was speechless (something I'm seldom afflicted with), then I said, trying to speak calmly, 'But it's a small area, only half a hectare, and it's been recorded as having a large selection of wildlife and plants. I was hoping to use it for the school field courses.'

He frowned and his lips curled. Even at that juncture I could read his mind. 'Pooh! What are a few insects and weeds compared with a nice extra bit of pasture.' I could understand his irritation. Here was this potty conservationist trying to upset his plans again.

At last he said, 'Well, I suppose it *is* a small area, but if you want me to set it aside for teaching your kids you'll have to see about the fencing and look after it yourself. Can't have my staff using up valuable time on it. You'd better see what Mr Brazenhall's got to say.'

'You won't spray it anyway, will you?' I asked anxiously.

'Who's going to cut all those dandelions and thistles? Don't want 'em seeding all over my fields.'

'I'll see about that,' I said. The College principal wasn't exactly pleased with my twisting his arm once again, but he said that if I could get a grant from somewhere to pay for the fencing, then perhaps the sheep could graze it that autumn. He obviously knew more about conservation than he usually let on. It still had to be cut beforehand to get it short enough for sheep. Daisy typed letters to all sorts of bodies to ask for a grant towards the cost of fencing and gates and at last we got a generous one from the Nature Conservancy Council.

It was my job to get some secondary-school students to set up the fence and put in the three-metre special gate and small access gate which would allow the sheep and cattle to be driven in and out of the area to graze it off in the autumn. Before that, I had to cut it myself by hand, using a scythe. It cost me two weeks' hard labour, an aching back and badly blistered hands, but it was worth it. Once or twice I imagined I saw a glint of binoculars through the captain's window and I hoped he understood and approved. I even got funds to put in a pipe to the nearest water main and install a cattle trough for the livestock to gain drinking water.

It was a bit of a shock when the College refused to graze it the following year on the grounds that it required extra work. However, a friendly farmer whom I'd advised over pond management agreed to put in a few beasts to graze it off. The grazing was essential to stop rank, coarse grasses taking over and dominating the shorter flowering plants. It wasn't long before I got some results and the crowning glory came two years later when the site was listed as a Grade B site of Botanical Interest by the Nature Conservancy Council.

I took the letter to show my friend the captain. Unfortunately I went too near teatime and had to take on board an even more luscious and highly calorific tea. It was worth it to see his gnarled countenance beaming with delight. He was delighted too when I told him that the previous week a secondary schoolboy on one of our courses working on a mammal-trapping project (the animals are caught for short periods in harmless containers and quickly released) had caught harvest mice— the first recorded in Clampshire for many years. He had done it on our little field.

Meanwhile my buffer zone project had produced real results over the years. Leaving an area untouched round the pond had made a measurable difference to pond-life. I had incorporated the results of this bit of research into a thesis on Farming and Wildlife which I submitted to Sanford University for an MSc. Copies of the thesis had been circulating and I had been asked to speak at a few colleges. Then one day I had received a letter from some top advisers of the Ministry of Agriculture who were based at the Royal Agricultural Centre in Stoneleigh (Warwickshire). I took it home to Clare.

'What do you think of this?' The letter invited me to act as consultant to a project similar to my buffer-zone project. This was a fully-controlled experiment on the prevention of fertilizer run-off reaching ponds. There was no offer of payment. Clare did not exactly give three cheers.

'Haven't you got more than enough on your plate already?'

'It's all part of the job,' I said airily. 'The kids from the schools can help and it'll be a wonderful way of getting conservation home to them.'

Clare's face registered resignation, but I knew that inside she felt it was an honour to be asked. Well, I think she did. I talked it over with Tommy Ferguson, the local Ministry of Agriculture, Fisheries and Food (MAFF) regional officer, to work out costs. It looked, at a rough guess, as though they would be at least a cool six thousand pounds a year. But the MAFF weren't footing the bill. The experiment required six ponds.

To reduce costs we proposed using ponds on a well-known organic farm in Shropshire, plus three ponds on the College farm, if *they* agreed, and one other pond belonging to a friendly farmer whose land was near the College. I knew he would agree! Then—bombshell! The Nature Conservancy Council turned down the idea flat as being statistically unworkable as a scientific study. They happily proposed digging *nine* identical ponds on the College estate in one area of uniform soil structure so that I could counter-check results. Why, of course, nothing could be simpler! There *was* just the small matter of the College being willing to allocate a two-hectare field. There seemed to be no end to my land-begging from the College.

And something had to be done about those costs. I needed a plan. The Nature Conservancy Council (NCC) offered a considerable amount of initial funding, and sent me to the Institute of Terrestrial Ecology to work with a brilliant statistician. He designed the layout of the nine ponds and their treatments. Following my simple idea of buffers, we worked out an equally simple buffer which any farmer could construct to prevent run-off and we aimed to use a certain water reed as an indicator of chemical residues, mainly nitrates and phosphates, in the water.

The most frustrating and insurmountable condition of the experiment was that the ponds would have to be left for one year to settle, for another year for unified treatment (the same treatment for each pond) and then for a further two years for different treatment for each group of ponds. The results would then be analyzed.

Before I knew where I was I'd booked myself and a field of two hectares of College land for four years. Some hope!

Now was the time to approach the College principal. I felt my stock was on a high after showing him the letter and also some research which confirmed my own conviction that cows feeding in fields with well-established hawthorn hedges were showing higher milk yields than cows in fields with wire fences, especially in windy areas.

Clampshire has a large number of days of strong wind in the growing season. Over the years, by using teams of schoolchildren, we had replanted five miles of hedgerow at the College. In the absence of comparative recordings it had not been possible to prove that we had improved the various yields but this research suggested hedgerows won over fences. Perhaps now was an opportune time to approach Mr Brazenhall, but I did it in fear and trembling.

It was now or never. Mr Brazenhall had got to be tackled. The plan and its financial backing were organized. Would he agree to allocate me two hectares of College farmland? I knocked at his door.

'Come in.'

I entered with what I hoped was a confident smile on my face. He was seated, head in hand, surrounded by papers. He looked up and I went to his desk.

My smile became stiff and mechanical as I read the

expression in his eyes. They said, quite plainly, 'Well, and what do you want this time?' His actual words were, 'Good morning Peter, what can I do for you?' Immediately I could see a direct approach was needed.

'You remember, some years back, that I was able to start that project to keep buffer zones round College ponds and I included it in my MSc thesis? Well, the MAFF have read it and invited me to act as a consultant on a fully-controlled research experiment on fertilizer run-off into ponds. It's been costed and a scheme worked out by the NCC. They will largely fund it, but I will have to get some sponsorship from other bodies to make up the shortfall. The scheme requires a series of small ponds to be dug on uniform land. Would it be possible for a piece of College land to be set aside for the work?'

His face would have made an interesting study for a physiognomist. His expression had changed in succession from patient boredom to lively interest and, with equal rapidity, to apprehension and then to opposition.

'How much land would it take?'

'Two hectares.' Surprisingly, there were signs of slight relief.

'How long would it have to be set aside?'

'Four years.'

'Four years! Good heavens, why so long?'

'The NCC say it would take one year to settle, one year for uniform treatment and the last two to give different treatments and analyze the results.'

By now repetition had made it sound like a few weeks to me, but not to Mr Brazenhall. He sat frowning and thinking.

'You say it'll be financed from outside?' I nodded, with my hopes rising.

'Well, if the governors and the farm manager agree, you can do it.'

'Thank *you*, sir!' I went out quickly before he could

change his mind. I fairly pranced into the Outdoor Centre office.

'Whoopee, Daisy, it's on!' Loyal soul, she beamed and did a thumbs-up.

'Now, we'll have to start raking in the cash. You know that letter I suggested? And the list of people we thought of sending it to? We'd better get busy.'

By coffee break Daisy had copies of the letter for the National Rivers Authority (NRA), the British Ecological Society (BES), the National Angling Foundation (NAF), and one or two other bodies I felt might be interested (including several fertilizer companies). At the end of a month we had the NRA, the BES and the NAF lined up, together with one or two small fertilizer companies—no response from the big ones. When we totted it up we found we could just cover the estimated six thousand pounds a year needed and it had been promised for the full four years. My attitude to officialdom took a distinct turn for the better.

I got the piece of land in a corner of the estate: clay soil; nice and flat; about two hectares in size. We started spending the grants—on fencing. Some of my secondary students enjoyed one or two outings from school putting them up. Then we began marking out the nine ponds in three rows. Each was circular, five metres in diameter and two metres deep. The project was explained to anybody who helped and it was remarkable the way these town kids got excited about it and were keen for it to succeed. My old friend, the round and bearded earth-mover who had dug the pond for the erstwhile 'destroyer', was hired with his excavator. He cut out the ponds with loving precision.

That winter the ponds quickly filled with land- and rain-water. I have some pictures taken from the air. It looked like a rash of spacecraft landing-sites. Now we needed some vegetation.

All our local reed-beds were in protected sites, so in

March I drove with two unemployed workers two hundred miles over the Pennines to a river in Yorkshire which the water authority was clearing with a drag-line. In snow and freezing conditions we hauled apart great masses of reeds from evil-smelling black river-mud, stuffed them into old fertilizer bags and heaved them into the back of the Land Rover. Then we drove back the two hundred miles in gathering darkness to get them to the College site. They had to be back in water within hours or they would perish.

We planted reeds in a row round the margin of all the ponds, and gradually we achieved plantings of reed grass and flote grass. After probing with metal rods, we located and blocked off sixty land drains in the field to make sure no fertilizer residue would get into the ponds through them.

For the specified two years the land was fertilized three times in the normal way, and our friendly local farmer cut the silage for us on several occasions, narrowly avoiding losing his silage machine in the deep, steep-sided ponds. He got his best yield during those years. No grazing was allowed, hence the fencing. Droppings would have complicated all our nitrogenous schemes. Meanwhile other pond plants were dug up and planted by my 'special conservation corps' of local Special Education kids. I had to record every step of the way.

Now was the time to use different treatments on the ponds. When the two years of equal treatment were up we killed all vegetation for a metre round the first three ponds and then began to fertilize normally around them. The second three were fertilized, but kept ordinary vegetation up to the edge and the last three had a three-metre zone round each pond kept fertilizer-free—the buffer zone.

At the time of writing we are now nearly through the fourth year. Despite bouts of being fed up with the whole project, there looms the possibility of a significant contribution to the whole business of fertilizer use in the future—both of manure and chemicals.

20

Farm School Successes

Alongside all the painstaking research projects, the Farm School visits were still proving successful—too successful sometimes. One morning as I entered the office Daisy raised her patient eyes from the last load of typed statistics.

'Peter, you haven't forgotten Potten High School, have you?'

I had. This was a long overdue visit. We were taking Farm School to an outlying and hitherto unvisited establishment.

'You know that East Midlands television are going to film it?'

I'd forgotten that too. I thanked the Lord inwardly for such a secretary.

A week later we were on the road again, with our usual menagerie of small and not-so-small animals. Before long we were in the big assembly hall with four hundred kids and it was going well. Really, it was a refreshing change from the pressures of the College farm. Even the animals behaved ... that is, until the advent of Neddy Wetherby, the TV producer for children's programmes.

Up until then, the cameras had given us very little bother, apart from the blazing lights getting in our eyes. I had just got a volunteer, a girl of about fourteen, in a pretty dress of bright cotton, who was holding Timothy, our prize piglet, in her arms.

In strode friend Neddy, wearing, of all things, a three-quarter length mink coat. I'll give it to him, he is good with children. After asking my permission, he got the girl positioned correctly and facing the cameras. But at that moment Timothy felt he had been embraced long enough and started to struggle. The girl clasped him more tightly.

'Smile, dear,' said Neddy. She smiled and, horror-stricken, Daisy and I watched as a stream of fluid left Timothy's undercarriage and soaked steadily down her dress. Her smile faded, but she held her position.

'Smile, *smile*, dear,' intoned Neddy. The flood had now reached her shoes and was forming an ever-widening pool on the floor, but smile she did.

All oblivious, Neddy said, 'I'll take him now, thank you dear.'

The piglet repeated his wriggle and, fatally, Neddy tightened *his* grasp. There was only one thing left to happen.

It did. An awesome, black, half-solid spurt shot out down Neddy's mink coat. He knew all about it this time, but, all credit to his professional stamina, he held Timothy still in a loving embrace and smiled, yes smiled, at the cameras. Daisy and I were aghast. We seized Timothy and, with profuse apologies, tried to clean up Neddy's ruined coat with the paper towels we always carried.

'Don't give it a thought,' he said in his warm Midlands accent, 'it'll teach me not to be so clever.'

Surprisingly, the demonstration at Potten High School was voted an astounding success by the Head and he invited us back. Daisy and I, with our animals safely loaded back into the trailer, left for home. We looked forward with some apprehension to the television version of the day's events. For the time being, ponds, fertilizers and fields could keep.

It seems that the Farm School visits made a deep and lasting impression on some children.

The telephone rang. It was Saturday evening and we were all having supper together.

'I'll get it,' I said.

A voice, rough and abrupt, spoke, 'You Mr 'amilton?'

'Yes, what can I do for you?'

'You collect animals?' I was cautious; what was coming?

'Ye-es, small animals maybe.'

I had visions of someone with another unwanted Bertram or a Great Dane to unload.

'Well, you come round 'ere, we got a loada frogs an' things, *if* you want 'em.'

This sounded promising. Besides, several amphibia are protected species. What on earth had this man got and where?

'What is your name and address?'

'You give me your word you won't do nothing, report us or something? I know we ain't supposed to 'ave certain things. It's my lad, he's mad on it—goes round collecting 'em, but we can't keep 'em, see? But we don't want no trouble—I'd rather chuck them down the loo or throw them in a ditch.'

'Don't worry, I promise I won't report you, but just give me your name and address.' After a moment's hesitation he did. His home was in a back street in Bentwich.

I arranged to call late on Monday when he was home from work.

The house was a down-at-heel semi. Mr Lockett took me out to the back garden, 'Y'see, it's our Bert, just mad on animals, any sort, but we can't afford to buy 'im nothing so 'e goes lookin' for 'em. Folk give 'im things too,' he added as we went down to the end of the garden where there was a motley collection of sheds.

'My boy's in the 'orspital, 'avin' 'is tonsils out at the moment, an' I reckon this lot are goin' ter peg out if nuffin's done for 'em.'

He opened one door after another and shone a torch in. For a moment I couldn't believe my eyes. Every shed was full of old buckets of every size. As his torch lit them up one by one I could see that they were alive with frogs, newts (including the increasingly rare, great crested variety) and at least half a dozen toads.

The boy must have known something about aquarian requirements because underneath the netting, which he'd fastened over the tops of the buckets, there was lots of oxygenating weed and small areas of stones had been piled up. There was a tap in one hut. The boy must have got water from that to keep the buckets fairly fresh.

'How long is it since he went into hospital?' I asked.

'Only got took in Sat'day,' he replied. ''Ad a cancellation, they said.'

'Well, you were right to call me, the whole lot would have died if they'd been left long. You know it's against the law to take those big long fellows?' I pointed at the crested newts.

'Guessed as much,' he said moodily. 'Couldn't stop 'im. 'S'all after 'im 'earing some bloke what come round 'is school with animals, said 'e wanted to be a conservationist or summin'.'

'What school does he go to?' I asked.

'Bentwich Primary.'

'Ahem, I'm afraid I must take some responsibility for his craze,' I said. 'I'm the bloke who came to his school.' He stared at me.

'But I didn't encourage them to go collecting wild things, only to try to take care of them. Anyway, if you'll help me get this lot into the back of my car I'll see they get into the right sort of home, in the College lake. When he's better he can come and see them and other live things we've got, if you'd like to bring him.'

He grinned. 'Great! I wouldn't mind seein' around myself.'

'Well, you'd be very welcome, and thanks for calling me.'

We carried the buckets, two by two, and stowed them with great care in the back of my estate car. I drove back to the College in the dark very slowly, but I still spilled a lot of the water on the floor of the car. One by one I gently poured the contents of the buckets into the College lake. I felt almost like a criminal, skulking there in the dark, until I thought of all those precious amphibian creatures which might now survive and proliferate. The frog, the toad and especially the great crested newt are now endangered species. I would have put the creatures in my own pond at home, but it was tiny, just a discarded cheese-vat from the College dairy which I had sunk in a flower-bed.

I went down to the College lake a few weeks later to be greeted by the 'coop—coop—coop' of mating toads. Five years previously I had requested that the head gardener's habit of clearing the underbrush below the trees near the lake to create 'a vista' should be halted. I was sure this practice had contributed to the decline of breeding birds in the vicinity of the lake. I had practically bribed three under-gardeners to aid me in making a survey of birds and now I could prove conclusively that the number of birds was steadily rising. Without this proof any further request would have fallen on deaf ears. Now I stood by the lake, listening to the early singing of the birds from their 'song-posts' in the trees around the pond, and the steady 'coop—coop' of the toads. It was a quiet moment in a whirl of activity.

Before the end of the spring term we had two more Farm Schools, one at College with primary-school teachers and the other at a distant comprehensive in a very deprived neighbourhood. I had been told that approximately seventy-five per cent of the parents were unemployed. I expected trouble at the comprehensive. Daisy and I had planned accordingly, with a foolproof exciting programme. That night as Clare and I said our prayers, we asked the Lord to see us through.

We drove in at about three o'clock and it was drizzling with rain. The Head, a tired-faced, grey-haired man, gave us a quick cup of tea and a biscuit in his room.

'I think I ought to warn you that these kids come from a poor area. There's a lot of broken marriages and strange family set-ups. Some of the children look as if they've been ill-treated but they will never admit it. I'm afraid that discipline is our worst problem. Watch out for one boy. He'll probably be sitting near the front. He usually wears a T-shirt with 'Manchester United' on the front. He's a troublemaker.' Daisy and I looked at each other. She surreptitiously gave me the merest wink and I felt better.

With surprisingly little trouble and a lot of help from the bigger boys we got all the animals into the assembly hall. The little piglet gave us most bother, but a strong lad held him firmly and put him in his cage with his partner on the platform where he quietly went to sleep.

I began by warning them sternly that animals could be dangerous, but if they behaved quietly and treated them with kindness they were perfectly all right. Silence fell. As I looked down on the smaller ones in the front, I could see some kids with scratches and bruises on their faces. There, in the second row, was a lad with a scowl on his face, a brush-cut and a T-shirt with 'Manchester United' on it.

'Now, I want a helper to hold some of the animals while I tell you about them. What about you, the Manchester United supporter?' I pointed at him. 'Want to come up?' He flushed bright red, but he proudly got to his feet and came up the steps on to the platform. There were some cheers (and a few boos). He was the best helper I had ever had. Somebody had trusted him at last and he

133

wasn't going to let them down. We ran through our routine, our little talk about animals, the land, flowers and trees—of which many of the children had seen precious little—and how God had made them so wonderful and different.

I showed them our beautiful cock, explaining how he, and all birds, have no feathers in their armpits so that they can spread their wings to keep cool in summer and tuck their heads under their wings at night to keep warm. I held him firmly and put his head under his wing to demonstrate this, which rather hurt his feelings but nothing else. Everything was going fine and I was interested to see that about fifteen or twenty men, probably unemployed dads, were standing attentively at the back of the hall. Suddenly there was a yell of fury, the swing doors burst open and a red-faced man strode in.

'Where's my son? I come to meet him and he ain't there!' He marched threateningly down the side aisle. But, without warning, his feet shot from under him and he fell with a thunderous crash. I could hear the bump as his head hit the parquet flooring. I guessed what had happened: our recalcitrant piggy had unwittingly come to our rescue by depositing a mantrap in the irate parent's path. The man lay for several seconds and then, with my help, gradually heaved himself to a sitting position. After rubbing his head for a few moments he allowed himself to be led out like a lamb by one of the larger and braver teachers.

As he left I noticed the Head slip through the doors and come in. I had caught glimpses of him listening outside throughout the proceedings. By now we had reached the stage when the children and parents were marshalled into groups to come up to pat and stroke the animals, which, as usual, behaved with dignified condescension towards their admirers.

At last we called it a day and, to my great pleasure, a tall lad, whom I learnt afterwards was the head boy, stood up and demanded silence.

'I think all you fellers and girls will agree we've had the best demonstration ever, so three cheers for Mr Hamilton and his helper! Hip Hip . . .'

As we closed the doors of the trailer the Head came up. 'Thank you, Mr Hamilton, for coming. I'm sorry about that parent, but he's all right. It was a very fine show, thank you both again.'

Back at the College farm I unloaded the last animal and went into the office where Daisy was clearing up.

'It didn't turn out quite as planned, Daisy.'

She smiled a tired smile. 'All's well that ends well,' she said.

I nodded. 'Thanks for your help.'

We switched out the lights and locked the office door.

21
The Best Laid Schemes

The day of the last farm visit of term dawned surprisingly bright and frosty. The primary-school teachers all arrived on time. One of our best heifers was due to calf any moment and we hoped we could stage a birth for their benefit. Of course, we had an alternative programme lined up if need be. The calving shed was pleasantly warm after the chill air outside, and the teachers were all marshalled in, their smart school gear covered by anoraks and wellies. Soon the head cowman was wrestling with a difficult labour. At last he got the calf's feet poking from the cow's rear end.

He gasped, 'Here, one of you take this rope, fix it like this round its feet and heave as I tell you, the rest of you get some buckets of water from that tap.' I don't know what they had bargained for, but those teachers were certainly getting their money's worth *and* something they wouldn't forget. While the cowman dived in to flex the calf's neck, one of the teachers, who was stronger than he looked, heaved on the rope. Gradually at first, and then with a rush, the slimy, little, elongated package slid out and was deposited carefully by the cowman on the straw. He cleared the calf's eyes and nostrils and the much-relieved mother was allowed to turn and complete the cleaning process with her tongue.

With the after-birth delivered, the cowman turned to

the goggle-eyed spectators and said, 'Well, how did you like that? Bit rough, eh? That's farming.' I noticed a hefty great teacher quietly wiping his eyes on the back of his hand. I wondered what he was thinking.

There was more in store. When I heard what was happening, I wondered if perhaps they'd had enough but I decided to risk it. I announced, 'The vet has come and he's going to perform an operation on a cow with a stomach obstruction. There's a cup of coffee in the canteen for anybody who doesn't want to see it.' But they came, all twelve of them.

A stall had been specially prepared and a tarpaulin laid. The observers could stand outside or sit on the steel fence between the stalls for a bird's-eye view. The cow had been anaesthetized with an intravenous injection. The beast had swallowed a hard object which was lodged in the abomasum stomach; the vet was perfectly confident in his diagnosis.

He plunged into the cow's side with nonchalant skill. It was a bit too nonchalant—the scalpel hit an artery and the blood spurted straight up to the ceiling before the vet could staunch it. There was a thud. There lay one fence-sitter in a faint, flat on his back on the straw of the next stall. He came to pretty quickly and we heaved him to his feet and escorted him in a wobbly state out of the cowshed. Before long a 50p coin was retrieved. The cow was trying to get up by the time we left. 'Bet it was a Scottish cow,' said a teacher of a hardier breed.

As I drove home to Clare and the children that afternoon, I thought of those lines of Burns which my Scottish dad was so fond of boring us with—'The best laid schemes of mice and men, gang aft agley'. How 'agley' can you get? Still, as Daisy had said, the term had ended well and I was thankful.

22

Green Wellies for All

By 1990, the world looked a 'greener' place. The 'Greens' were a growing power in the land and the ozone layer and greenhouse effect were subjects of everyday conversation. For five years the Centre had organized a widely-advertised course on 'Creating Wildlife Habitats on Farms and in Gardens'. And now I was to meet the latest group to attend this course.

It was a privilege to bring together such an assorted bunch of enthusiasts—smallholders, businesspeople, farmers, students, lecturers, agricultural contractors and just ordinary people interested in conservation. The course was taking place at the College during the vacation, and was to run for three days. I felt slightly apprehensive at the beginning of the course—a potent combination of interests could sometimes spark off some verbal fireworks.

On the first night, to break the ice, the course members were all invited to stand up and tell us about their jobs. It was illuminating.

'I'm the editor of a national organic smallholders' magazine,' said a dark-haired woman. 'I live in Northern Ireland and I am fundamentally opposed to British Nuclear Fuels dumping their nuclear waste in the Irish Sea.'

Next to her was a middle-aged lady with blonde hair

and blue-rimmed spectacles. 'I am a physicist in British Nuclear Fuels and I see nuclear energy as a major clean source of power into the 21st Century,' she said quietly. There was a pregnant silence. It was broken by a pale young man who let us know he was a vegan.

Then there was a poultry farmer, a hearty young countryman if ever there was one. He rose, 'Oi'm gettin' excellent results from spreadin' poultry muck on a pasture. We get the most wonderful wild flowers, but it's a shame to see them go when we coots the 'ay.'

A burly red-faced man announced that he was a policeman. 'I've come across from Northampton on a bicycle—my little bit towards cutting down pollution from car fumes. I'm hoping to pick up some hints on encouraging wildlife.' He added quietly, 'I have a local authority nature reserve garden but there are a few species of birds and animals not there yet.'

He was sitting next to a small man who was chain-smoking, in spite of the 'no smoking' notice. I had happened to see his car, a big Ford, and was intrigued by the rear window, which was almost completely covered with stickers: 'Protect the Whale', 'Greenpeace', 'Friends of the Earth', 'Earth Watch', 'Ban the Bomb', 'Worldwide Fund for Nature', 'Ban Battery Eggs', 'Chickens' Lib' and 'Compassion in World Farming'. 'Anti Blood Sports' was just fitted into one corner. Towards the end of this get-together he stood up, stubbing out his cigarette on the table desk, and said, 'I have just succeeded in purchasing a fairly large estate and I wish to convert it to wildlife management and I hope to get some hints from this course. I have in mind the creation of a donkey and goat sanctuary.'

The poultry farmer said, quite loudly, 'The best thing yer can do with goats is kill 'em and eat 'em!'

The young vegan got up and walked out of the lecture room.

A man who could have helped the estate owner was a

chap announcing that he was a landscape gardener who was there to get some ideas for water features. He wrote to me after the course was over, saying he had been so inspired about protecting wildlife that he had returned home and had immediately started to create a pond along the lines we had discussed.

The estate owner could also have benefited from the services of the man who spoke last, who simply said he was a drainage contractor. By the end, the contractor had become so inspired about digging ponds for wildlife instead of draining land that he told me he intended to try to create them on all the farms he went to. He also said he would support creating areas for wildlife by suggesting the planting of woods and hedgerows.

Lastly, a tall young man with a handsome brown face stood up. 'I am from Nigeria. I am an agriculturalist and I am a Christian.' There was complete silence. 'I am here to learn some new things which will help our country to use its land well and not spoil God's gift to us. Thank you.'

It looked as if we were in for stirring times. I hoped the eight lecturers would dilute the mixture a bit.

The programme included visits to farms around Clampshire run with concern for the environment in mind and also to a number of gardens. The next morning I noticed that 'nuclear fuel' was sharing a seat (by sheer chance) on the coach with 'nuclear opposition' and that an icy silence reigned. But the frigid atmosphere gradually warmed up over the day, as the nuclear physicist admitted that she hoped to retire to a wee cottage in the Lake District. Both women became so enthralled by the created wildlife habitats, ponds, species-rich meadows, woods and hedges we visited that discussing them together welded a true friendship.

After a very shaky start, it was amazing how peace broke out as more friendships were established. As usual on these occasions, my own ego got a bit of a knocking, and so did those of the experts among the lecturers. On several occasions we were completely stumped over the identification of a moth or a bird or a rare plant. In the party was one boy of sixteen. Strictly speaking he was two years under the minimum age accepted, but he had been so keen we had let him come. He had just left school and had no official qualification whatsoever, but it became quickly apparent that in his quiet way he showed more knowledge as a naturalist than the rest of us 'experts' put together. He was a 'natural' in every sense!

By the last night it seemed that the study of God's creation had drawn us all together. I tried to sum things up. We talked of pollution and one of the folk said quite openly 'It's nothing more nor less than sin.' I went on, 'Don't you feel that *God* is the Creator of this wonderful world? And haven't we the responsibility, not as owners but as tenants, to manage our patch as an example to the rest? He will give us the strength and determination to do it! Doing nothing will be even worse than sitting and wringing our hands.'

The estate owner said humbly as we broke up for coffee, 'Thanks Peter, you'll convert us all yet!'

As I shook his hand I said, 'Not a chance, Eric, only God can do that!'

The next morning I waved goodbye to the course members—a motley bunch drawn together by a common interest. And I thought of all the thousands of people, children and adults alike, who had come to the Centre over the years. And I thought of all the steps we had taken together towards conserving our environment—the school visits, the Farm School, the courses for adults, students, and sixth-formers. There was pond reclamation, hedgerow planting, teacher training, adult education ...

It was about time I had another brilliant idea!

Peter Hamilton speaks and lectures widely in the UK. He can be contacted by writing to:

PO Box 26
Sevenoaks
Kent
TN13 2EL

More titles from LION PUBLISHING for you to enjoy

GRIEF CHILD Lawrence Darmani	£4.99 ☐
SONS AND BROTHERS Elizabeth Gibson	£2.99 ☐
OLD PHOTOGRAPHS Elizabeth Gibson	£3.99 ☐
TALIESIN Stephen Lawhead	£3.99 ☐
MERLIN Stephen Lawhead	£3.99 ☐
ARTHUR Stephen Lawhead	£3.99 ☐
THE BREAKING OF EZRA RILEY John L. Moore	£5.99 ☐
CANDLE IN THE STRAW Clare Wyatt	£3.99 ☐

All Lion paperbacks are available from your local bookshop or newsagent, or can be ordered direct from the address below. Just tick the titles you want and fill in the form.

Name (Block letters) PAULINE McNEILL

Address 41 ARGYLL Ave. LARNE,
Co. ANTRIM. N. IRELAND
BT40-2JX

Write to Lion Publishing, Cash Sales Department, PO Box 11, Falmouth, Cornwall TR10 9EN, England.

Please enclose a cheque or postal order to the value of the cover price plus:

UK: 80p for the first book, 20p for each additional book ordered to a maximum charge of £2.00.

OVERSEAS INCLUDING EIRE: £1.50 for the first book, £1.00 for the second book and 30p for each additional book.

BFPO: 80p for the first book, 20p for each additional book.

Lion Publishing reserves the right to show on covers and charge new retail prices which may differ from those previously advertised in the text or elsewhere, and to increase postal rates in accordance with the Post Office.